Reaching Deeper

Also by Laurel Hallman

Living by Heart, a video conversation with Harry Scholefield and Laurel Hallman. *By Heart Video,* Publisher 1996.

Living by Heart, a workbook to accompany the video. *By Heart Video,* Publisher, 2003.

Reaching Deeper

Selected Sermons by Laurel Hallman

Xlibris - Philadelphia, PA

Library of Congress Control Number: 2008902027
ISBN: Hardcover   978-1-4363-2536-3
                 Softcover   978-1-4363-2535-6

Cover art: Deep Down by Wainer Vaccari
Back photo by Peter Poulides
Cover design and interior art by Kathryn Yingling

"All Beliefs" (excerpt) reprinted with the permission of David Rankin.

"First Lesson", from LETTER FROM A DISTANT LAND by Philip Booth, copyright (c) 1957 by Philip Booth. Used by permission of Viking Penguin, a division of Penguin Group (USA) Inc.

"The Rowing Endeth", from THE AWFUL ROWING TOWARD GOD by Anne Sexton. Copyright (c) 1975 by Loring Conant, Jr., Executor of the Estate of Anne Sexton. Reprinted by permission of Houghton Mifflin Harcourt Publishing Company. All rights reserved.

"You, Neighbor God", by Rainer Maria Rilke, Translated by Babette Deutsch, from POEMS FROM THE BOOK OF HOURS, copyright (c) 1941 by New Directions Publishing Corp. Reprinted by permission of New Directions Publishing Corp.

"Practicing the Scales of Rejoicing" reprinted with the permission of Richard Gilbert.

"Wild Geese", from DREAM WORK by Mary Oliver. Copyright © 1986 by Mary Oliver. Used by permission of Grove/Atlantic, Inc.

This book was printed in the United States of America.
To order additional copies of this book, contact:
Xlibris Corporation
1-888-795-4274
www.Xlibris.com
Orders@Xlibris.com
47235

This book is dedicated to the members of congregations
I have loved in Bloomington, Indiana and Dallas, Texas.
Their lives have said so much more than I could ever imagine.

Contents

 Introduction

Those of us who have long been familiar with Laurel Hallman's personal energy and quietly intense focus of purpose may easily call up a vision evoked by her self-description as fundamentalist high-school student—president of the Pep Club, carrying her Bible on top of her school books, not dancing, preparing to become a missionary, and striving "to be popular for Jesus." What she drew most profoundly from her childhood immersion in "the love of Jesus and the judgment of God" was an intellectual integrity that would summon her inexorably away from the certainties of her inherited faith, into a persistent engagement with the open-ended possibilities of meaning in Unitarian Universalist community. Ultimately, it would draw her to a life of leadership and service in our congregations. The dogmas are gone, but the urgency of soul remains. This collection of sermons demonstrates that for Laurel, the use of the religious imagination is more than a style preference or a rhetorical flourish; it is a moral and spiritual imperative.

The ability to conjure metaphors, either verbally through poetry, visually in the mind's eye, or in narratives that encode a larger story, is what makes possible our most meaningfully human lives. It informs the success of our relationships, from the intimacies of marriage, to the covenant community of memory and promise in the local congregation, to our responsible citizenship in the global context, and our ability to imagine our place in the universal order of things. The religious imagination is what sustains us individually in moments of personal distress and public tragedy, as well as through the discouragements and challenges of working to make real the world we envision together.

In *Images for Our Lives*, Laurel recounts that "I recently spoke to our Adult Sunday School Class in Dallas on the topic 'Why I am Not a Theist'. They packed the room to hear what I had to say, because of course they thought I was. Why did they think I was a theist? Because I use the word God. Because I pray in the midst of the worship service. I was embarrassed a bit myself, to find that

I had failed to make the distinction that the use of metaphors and poetry and scripture has to do with religious imagination, and not with one theological category or another . . . Let me quickly explain that by poetry I mean words and phrases, even whole narrative stories that point beyond themselves to the depth of human experience. I believe that poetry is scripture. I believe that scripture is poetry."

This commitment to understanding the theological enterprise as properly the realm of imaginative creativity has a double-sided implication for those of us who profess the living tradition of a free faith. In the first place, it is our responsibility never to allow the metaphors of our spiritual engagement to freeze hard into literalism. Part of the task of our practice is continually to break open the stories and the images into paradox and confusion, so that new meanings may take root in them. In *Is God A Christian?* Laurel writes, "The metaphors, the structures, the religions which begin as new ways of knowing and being known, quickly become barriers to the very knowing we seek. The minute some helpful image, some word of truth becomes etched for all time into the glass which had been a clear window through which the light passed—the minute the word becomes etched, our vision is obscured, the truth distorted, our perception marred." The religious imagination must ever bring new perspectives and possibilities to our encounter with ultimacy.

At the same time, it is incumbent upon us, in our freedom, to plumb the existing stories, images, and phrases of humanity's religious heritage for the living wisdom that they may still have to offer about the human condition. In *You're Not Crazy*, Laurel assures the doubtful church-goer, "As crazy as it may seem, church may be the place for new melodies, and new country to be revealed. If you can admit that there might be a silence worth listening to, some truth worth waiting for, some new life worth your yearning—that not only when you show up here, we have to let you in, but in some ultimate way, when you show up for Life, Love embraces you. Then let me tell you, brother and sister, you are not crazy. You are in the right place." In this place, we align ourselves with the efforts of all our forebears to report honestly about their experience of the sacred, and seek to unpack the truth they told through the sympathy of our own religious imaginations. To dismiss unexamined what they cherished is to impoverish our own spiritual journeys, and to break faith with the theological creativity of our tradition.

Not only is the fluent use of metaphor essential to a grounding and fulfilling personal spiritual life, as those who have connected to the *Living By Heart* materials have learned; it is also indispensable to the integrity of a faith community. It is the work of shared religious imagination that calls us out of mere self-concern, and into institutions that have a vision to announce. The purpose of the church, Laurel tells us in *More Than Enough*, is to create the story of a people, a tribe that stands for something; "The power of freedom, to open the mind and heart, to break open the bonds of literalism and oppression, to create a place where people can find their way out of the desert, out of the wilderness, where people can find their way home." This authentic religious community must abide in the creative tension of metaphorical paradox, confusion, and discernment, for only in this state is it alive, with the collective imagination at work as it ought to be. In such a community, stories and images arise to energize people with hope and courage, then begin to harden into literalism, and are broken open to new possibilities by the continual re-imagination of their shared meanings.

This is a process not unique to Unitarian Universalism, and these sermons illustrate a religious awareness that transcends narrow denominational boundaries. The poetry of faith, in which religious language speaks with confidence in the power and truth of metaphor, is a heritage that is shared by many different theological and confessional perspectives. Laurel offers it with assurance and grace, grounded in her own spiritual identity, but calling us all to a wider range of connections with our many diverse companions on this journey. This volume is a contribution to the dialogue among writers of the spirit for a new millennium.

In the end, Laurel dares to propose that the work of theological creativity may be necessary even to the divine itself. Perhaps, in an existence as tenuous and contingent as our own, that which is holy depends upon the persistence of our religious imagination. "What if we have this thing completely turned around?" she asks at the close of *Is God A Christian?* "[What if] the ultimate ground of being needs our images, our stories, our frames to know him/herself? God may need us to name the thousand names, to be imaged as a he, as a she, or imaged as a burning bush, as the scientific method, as an infinite number of names, because for whatever reasons, those are the only way he/she/it/they can know him/her/it/themselves. What if, however flawed, religion is a gift to God, because God needs religion as a way of knowing and being known?" And she concludes wryly, "If this is so, it is too bad, for we are not very good at it." But having been summoned into the richly explored images of the sermons offered here, we are better than we were.

Kendyl Gibbons
Minneapolis, 2008

# Foreword

I understood the power of preaching as I sat as a child listening to what we now call *hellfire and brimstone* sermons. What I heard was captivating, and at the same time found its place in my deepest fears and longings.

When I became a Unitarian Universalist I began to see a way that preaching could be just as captivating, and also liberate me and give my life meaning and purpose.

The day I understood that religious language is metaphorical, not literal, I was freed to reach deeper into the heart of religion to find the truths I needed to hear, but which had been kept from me by literal doctrinal interpretations. I began to see the religious imagination as a path to depth, and began to walk freely in a world of poetry and scripture, unencumbered by logical positivist questions of "did it happen?" or "do you believe it?" Truth was to be found at a place apart from those concerns.

My D.Min. Thesis, *The Uses of Religious Imagination in Sermons*, helped me discipline myself to find a language that went beyond the common languages of psychology and politics, efficiency and technology—to preach depth of meaning and purpose. In it, I wrote, "The symbols to which we turn are often unable to represent reality when 'depth speaks to depth.'"

I have been fortunate to serve two wonderful churches where I was given the freedom of the pulpit to practice what I had learned. The members of my congregations in Bloomington, Indiana and in Dallas, Texas, carved out my ministry with their very lives. I had to take into account not only what I thought about things, but how it was for them. I had to take into account what had happened to all of us together.

I preached my way through the suicide at Christmas of the Treasurer of our church, a week when there were seven deaths, a Sunday when the chosen topic was *Part of My Soul Went with Him* by Winnie Mandela—which turned out to be the same week my partner ended our relationship. (It was ironic that later, after Nelson Mandela was released from prison, he and Winnie divorced.)

I have preached following the death of my Father, the marriage of my Son, the birth of my Granddaughter—when I admit I indulged my own need to share my life, whether in any kind of larger context, or not.

I have always preached with a sense of inadequacy, praying that the spoken word would find some place in the hearts of my listeners.

I have preached my way through the AIDS epidemic, when there was always at least one person in the congregation whose presence reminded us that death was near. I preached (inadequately) following 9/11 when there were few words to be said.

This collection began with the insistence from some of the members that there be a collection of sermons from my years in the Dallas church. When Jane Ramberg volunteered to lead the project, it became possible. When members of the congregation were asked to submit their 'favorites', they often came to us with phrases or stories that had 'stuck' for years, but weren't connected to any one sermon. Most of the time we could find the one they remembered. Not always.

When I felt unable to give any direction to the project, at Jenny Weil's suggestion, Jane gathered an informal group of people who had things to say about my sermons. Their conversation that night—facilitated by Jenny—opened me to the currents that ran through the sermons, and the possibility that we could have a collection of some of them. What I had been doing on my own became possible in the midst of that group. Thanks to Gayle Watson, Jenny Weil, Jane Ramberg, Paul Crabtree, Charles McMullen, Jim Crawford, and Lee Taft for being there that night.

Jane said one day, "What about that painting you have talked about so often? Do you think we could put it on the cover?" At first I was skeptical. A colleague, Douglas Wilson, had sent me a post card of the wonderful painting "Deep Down" by Wainer Vaccari after I had preached the sermon *Like a Pool Into Which We Plunge* at the Unitarian Universalist Ministers Convocation in Hot Springs, Arkansas in 1995. Douglas said, "This picture reminded me of your sermon." I was astounded. Without words, it said *exactly* what I felt about preaching: I was continually being invited to dive, and to dive into the depths. I always had a certain amount of anxiety about writing, and suddenly I understood why. It wasn't performance anxiety. It was the anxiety of diving. I have kept that postcard on my desk since the day I received it. Could we get permission to put it on the cover of the book? Jane said she'd try. She found the artist's gallery in Italy. They asked for my sermon to explain why she needed permission to use the painting. They sent word she could call the artist, not remembering to mention he spoke only Italian. Trying French, Jane and Vaccari communicated enough to get his permission and make the necessary arrangements. I am thrilled that it is on the cover of this collection of my work.

These sermons span a period of 20 years. I have chosen not to update the language or "fix" them so I would seem wiser than I was at the time. They stand as they were; sometimes flawed, sometimes with surprising insight that was ahead of what I actually knew.

There are so many people to thank. First, my two congregations. Then my preaching mentors, John Wolf, Roy Phillips and Harry Scholefield, among so many other wonderful preachers in our tradition who have shaped me. Then Jane Ramberg, without whom this book wouldn't have happened. Then Paul Crabtree who scanned old sermons into a form we could work with, helped edit sermons and obtained copyright permissions. Then Tanis Weiss who did bibliographic research and fine tuned the editing. Then Katherine Yingling who added her artistic talent to the layout and motifs throughout the book. Then Janny Strickland, who generously made the project possible. And finally, my gratitude to the spirit of life which created, each week, out of the chaos of experience and hope, something which I took into the pulpit and preached, hoping that the word spoken would heal, challenge, and bless all who heard it.

Laurel Hallman
Dallas, 2008

Is God A Christian?
April 17, 1988

I first heard the Rilke poem recited by Joseph Sittler, who recited it by heart in a class I took from him. He was elderly and blind, and taught the class on Religion and Literature from his memory. I was transfixed. This sermon came out of my fascination with the poet's idea that images can become a wall between that which is so near to us and our deepest selves. I wanted to take the wall which many have built with the images in Christianity and see if I could break it open. The ending surprised even me. LH

You, Neighbor God
By Ranier Maria Rilke

> You, neighbor God, if sometimes in the night
> I rouse you with loud knocking, I do so
> only because I seldom hear you breathe;
> I know: you are alone.
> And should you need a drink, no one is there
> to reach it to you, groping in the dark.
> Always I hearken. Give but a small sign.
> I am quite near.
>
> Between us there is but a narrow wall,
> and by sheer chance; for it would take
> merely a call from your lips and from mine
> to break it down,
> and that all noiselessly.
>
> The wall is builded of your images.
>
> They stand before you hiding you like names,
> and when the light within me blazes high
> that in my inmost soul I know you by,
> the radiance is squandered on their frames.
> And then my senses, which too soon grow lame,
> exiled from you, must go their homeless ways.[1]

Is God a Christian? I've had more comments this week about this title than for any sermon I've announced since I've been with you. Is God a Christian? Some of you have worried aloud that I might say 'yes.' Others have imagined what might happen if there was a reporter here this week and I said 'no.'

Actually, there is a question I must ask before I ask if God is a Christian. And that is, "Is God religious?" My thinking for this sermon began, in fact,

3

with someone I know saying—people say these kinds of things offhandedly to ministers—"God isn't religious. People are religious. God doesn't need to be religious."

At the time, I was struck with the rightness of the remark. For we humans, after all, are the ones who light candles, tell stories and say prayers. Religion is, after all, a very human enterprise. It seems absurd to think of God, if there is a God, making up some of the things that pass for religion in our time.

Some would say that is all that needs to be said. Some would say "End. Fini. All she wrote. Let us be about our business and not worry ourselves with God *or* religion. God, if there be a God, isn't religious, and we don't need to be either." All well and good. We could leave it there. But, it is not enough for me to look at the failures of some and say the whole religious endeavor is wrong-minded. Besides that, I've tried to not be religious, and I can't do it. I don't think it's because I'm a minister, either. Because, all absurdity aside—all pomp, all literalism, all misuse of religion for self-serving purposes—there is still something in the human experience that yearns for meaning, for purpose, for a way to relate to the ground of existence. A way to know and be known.

In *Teaching a Stone to Talk*, Annie Dillard, says, "What have we been doing all these centuries but trying to . . . raise a peep out of anything that isn't us? What is the difference between a cathedral and a physics lab? Are not they both saying 'Hello'? We spy on whales and on interstellar radio objects; we starve ourselves and pray till we're blue."[2] That is the religious impulse. Most basic to our human existence. And so, it seems, we humans conjecture, imagine, form images of how it might be to know, to be known; to respond and be responded to.

The religious experience is like being on a great sea, lost (it is said) and then, after months of floating, receiving an olive branch from a dove, and knowing the shore is in sight. It's like seeing a burning bush. It's as if we're in a great wrestling match in which we, like Jacob, must wrestle with an angel for our blessing. It's all emptiness which, if truly comprehended, becomes fullness beyond understanding. It's like the flame in a chalice. It's a momentary vision of truth, of justice. It's the surprise of love. It's saying 'hello,' and maybe once in a while hearing or sensing a 'hello' in return.

I imagine that from the beginning of time the religious enterprise has consisted mainly of people saying, "It's like this . . . and this and this," struggling to put into words, into images, that which cannot be grasped, cannot be truly represented, but only alluded to. Saying 'hello' in one way or another, trying to make tangible some small knowing, some small sense of having been known, writing it down, telling it in story, in hopes that by doing so someone else might have the same, or a similar experience.

"It's a gift," they said one day. "A child given to us who is wiser than anyone we have ever known. He grew up to be a great teacher, a teller of stories that carried great meaning. New ways to live. New ways to think about life. Beyond laws, beyond rules. Ruled, rather, by love. His teachings drawn from the very relationships the people knew. He said that God is like a Father, the church is like a Bride, everyone is Brother and Sister to everyone. All of us children. He spoke of images of religion—not as far-away ideas or abstract thoughts—but known in the very things the people knew and lived. He spoke in metaphors—even said that was what he was doing—so people could better understand what he was trying to say. And when he died a martyr's death, his life became a metaphor itself—a story of being known even in a moment of ultimate betrayal, failure and darkness."

All this is to say—for I haven't forgotten the original question—that God may be represented by Christianity. Christianity may have arisen out of a very real sense of knowing and having been known. But it is not all knowing. Only representative.

The only way we could say that God is a Christian is to tell the story of the seven blind men and the elephant. You know the story. Seven blind men are standing around an elephant. Each is reporting what he feels. "An elephant is snake-like" one says, touching the trunk, "a large curved snake." "An elephant is like the trunk of a tree," says another, wrapping his arms around a leg. "A vine," says another feeling the tail, "a tufted vine." And so on. Each quite sure that the portion of reality he was experiencing was the totality.

The only way we can say that God is a Christian is to say that long ago some blind men—for finally, we're all blind—had a phenomenal experience with a man, and with events around the life and death of that man. They were empowered by their experiences, by the feeling that—after centuries of calling out, of shouting 'hello' to emptiness—God had answered in human form. God had spoken. They gathered and wrote and taught and did their best to convey what they had seen. And they called it Christian.

Is God a Christian? Maybe. Maybe they did grasp some portion of reality not known before. Maybe they did capture—in story, metaphor and image—some small part of what it means to be human and divine at the same time. Maybe what they called Christian is a way of seeing the elephant—containing some truth, but truth that is limited. Maybe a portion of the light—of truth, of the understanding, the light which warms our faces when we call out in our yearning—does stream back at us in ways we can call Christian.

It would be great if our relationship with the ground of life, the center of existence—call it what you will, call it God—were easily understood and known through one simple lens. But, for reasons I do not understand, it doesn't seem to be so. We seem to be destined to know our deepest selves, know those closest to us, know that which knows us, in ways that are for the most part veiled and obscure. Such knowing is elusive.

And, too, the metaphors, the structures, the religions which begin as new ways of knowing and being known, quickly become barriers to the very knowing we seek. The minute some helpful image, some word of truth becomes etched for all time into the glass that had been a clear window through which the light passed—at that moment our vision is obscured, the truth distorted, our perception marred. This is the power of Rilke's words. "Between us there is a narrow wall," he says. "The wall is builded of your images." And then "the radiance is squandered on their frames."

We yearn. We call out, trying to get a peep out of something that is not ourselves. Something that will reflect who we are, who we can be. Then, like the blind men fumbling in the dark, we discover we are standing in front of an elephant. And we say, 'this is it!' We are comforted—until we discover that the elephant is much larger than the trunk, the tail, the leg we have grasped. "And so we go our homeless ways," Rilke says.

But that is only true if we reject understandings because they are, inevitably, limited. For, if once we find them too small (if we find that the God we understood was not God but some small representation that bears only the slightest resemblance to a larger truth) and we then feel we must throw out the whole enterprise (because it is not the whole of it, the whole truth of it), then we would cease from all human quests. The windows through which we see our natural world. The windows of scientific inquiry. Shutter them. Close them off, because we can know so little and can be so wrong. Darken the windows of self-knowledge because we can delude ourselves so easily. Pull the shades on the windows of relationships because we never know enough, never allow ourselves to be known enough. Because so often our perceptions of even those closest to us are so surprisingly limited. Shutter your house. Close the drapes. Sit in darkness, if you believe the windows through which you view the world are too small, too distorted or too limited to help.

God is not a Christian. We are the ones with the windows to the ultimate, through which we see and are seen. Christianity has been an important frame for many of us, a window-frame through which we began to understand some things about religion, began to name our yearning, began to give words to our knowing, our sense of being known. It is a window frame, a piece of glass that is ground to whatever clarity it has from the very stuff of our lives, not God's being.

Finally, all we have are the flawed, tattered and warped frames which we hold up to capture what light we can. Looking out, calling out, hoping for some small sign, be it from a whale, or interstellar space. Finally, we can only live in gratitude that God doesn't need to be a Christian. For a time at least, the frame, the window that we call Christianity has given us some light. It has been, in Yeats' words, "dappled with shadow"[3] as all such lights are. But we can be grateful for whatever little glimmers of light we have received.

God is not a Christian. God is not even religious. He/she/it doesn't need to be. But, we do. We need to call out, in our way, trying to raise a peep out of the universe. Reminded of the light, even in our darkness. Groping to know the elephant, even in our blindness. And, perhaps at times sensing we have connected somehow, be it through the window of Christianity, or some other traditional window of religion, or a new framework—a frame from the work, the journey, the quest of our own lives.

God is not a Christian any more than he/she/it is a scientist. Those are our ways of knowing. Gifts, magnificent gifts. From God? Who knows. But as long as darkness reminds us of light, as long as we are able to hold up our window frames to the darkness and see light, we can be grateful.

This is the end of today's sermon as I originally imagined it. But there is one more thing I want to say. This occurred to me as I wrote, a startling thought that I must add. Pure conjecture—an addendum, an epilogue.

What if God needs those windows as much as we do? What if God, for reasons we can't explain, is as limited as we are? What if that peep we are yearning for is yearning back? What if we are God's prayer? What if *we* are images (however flawed) of ultimate truth? What if the frames we hold up reveal as much the other direction as they do ours? What if we are the ones who bring truth into tangible reality—that God can't.

What if we are not so much the witnesses to God's work, God's power, but rather God is that which witnesses our work, our power. What if we have this thing completely turned around? That the ultimate ground of our being needs our images, our stories, our frames to know him/herself? God may need us to name the thousand names—to be imaged as a he, a she, or as a burning bush, the scientific method, or as an infinite number of names—because, for whatever reasons, those are the only way he/she/it/they can know him/her/it/themselves. What if, however flawed, religion is a gift *to* God because God needs religion as a way of knowing and being known?

If that is so, it is too bad, because we're not very good at it. But that might be the way it is. Or some small window into the way it is. Maybe.

Cheap Grace
June 5, 1988

I wrote this sermon in a state of shock. Following minor surgery on May 9th, I had become inexplicably paralyzed on my left side from the hip down. I remember practicing moving into the Chancel as smoothly as possible on my crutches, and then leaning on the pulpit to preach this sermon. It was unclear at that point whether I would be able to continue my ministry. My congregation held its collective breath for at least a year until I literally 'got back on my feet'. At times I felt like Job, at times like Jacob who wrestled with an angel for his blessing. People told me I'd be a better minister because of it. Am I? Maybe. LH

Sorrow and Joy
By Dietrich Bonhoeffer

Sorrow and joy,
striking suddenly on our startled senses,
seem, at the first approach, all but impossible
of just distinction one from the other,
even as frost and heat at the first keen contact
burn us alike.

Joy and sorrow,
hurled from the height of heaven in meteor fashion,
flush in an arc of shining menace o'er us.
Those they touch are left
stricken amid the fragments
of their colourless, usual lives.

Imperturbable, mighty,
ruinous and compelling,
sorrow and joy
—summoned or all unsought for—
processionally enter.
Those they encounter
they transfigure, investing them
with strange gravity
and a spirit of worship.

Joy is rich in fears;
sorrow has its sweetness.
Indistinguishable from each other
they approach us from eternity,
equally potent in their power and terror.

From every quarter
mortals come hurrying,
part envious, part awe-struck,
swarming, and peering
into the portent,
where the mystery sent from above us
is transmuting into the inevitable
order of earthly human drama.

What, then, is joy? What, then, is sorrow?
Time alone can decide between them,
when the immediate poignant happening
lengthens out to continuous wearisome suffering,
when the laboured creeping moments of daylight
slowly uncover the fullness of our disaster,
sorrow's unmistakable features.

Then do most of our kind,
sated, if only by the monotony
of unrelieved unhappiness,
turn away from the drama, disillusioned,
uncompassionate.

O you mothers and loved ones—then, ah, then
comes your hour, the hour for true devotion.
Then your hour comes, you friends and brothers!
Loyal hearts can change the face of sorrow,
softly encircle it with love's most gentle
unearthly radiance.[1]

An excerpt from *The Prophet*
By Kahlil Gibran

Then a woman said, Speak to us of Joy and Sorrow.
    And he answered:
    Your joy is your sorrow unmasked.
    And the selfsame well from which your laughter rises was
oftentimes filled with your tears.
    And how else can it be?
    The deeper that sorrow carves into your being, the more joy you
can contain.

Is not the cup that holds your wine the very cup that was burned in the potter's oven?

And is not the lute that soothes your spirit, the very wood that was hollowed with knives?

When you are joyous, look deep into your heart and you shall find it is only that which has given you sorrow that is giving you joy.

When you are sorrowful look again in your heart, and you shall see that in truth you are weeping for that which has been your delight.

Some of you say, "Joy is greater than sorrow," and others say, "Nay, sorrow is the greater."

But I say unto you, they are inseparable. Together they come, and when one sits alone with you at your board, remember that the other is asleep upon your bed.

Verily you are suspended like scales between your sorrow and your joy.

Only when you are empty are you at standstill and balanced.

When the treasure-keeper lifts you to weigh his gold and his silver, needs must your joy or your sorrow rise or fall.[2]

Jimmy Swaggart and I are back!

The circumstances of our departures from our respective pulpits are somewhat different, needless to say. Swaggart, you will remember, was ordered to seek counseling and refrain from preaching for a year by his denomination, the Assembly of God, after the revelation that he had committed moral improprieties. In defiance of that order, he left the denomination of his ordination and resumed his pulpit last week. My understanding is that he is back on television today.

I, on the other hand, as many of you know, came out of anesthesia from a routine day surgery almost a month ago to discover that my sciatic nerve had been damaged, causing numbness and paralysis of my left leg. Instead of returning home that afternoon as planned, I spent eight days in the hospital, and the time since going to physical therapy and getting my bearings, physically and otherwise.

It's been an amazing time for both of us, Jimmy Swaggart and me. He says that the revelations of his visit to a prostitute precipitated a "struggle so intense I despaired of my life and prayed for God to take it." But now, forgiven by God, he says he has laid his guilt at the cross and will never, ever look back. Making a new start, 5,000 people came to hear him speak of how he had been forgiven and how much stronger his ministry will be.

The prognosis is not so clear for me. The neurologist says four to six weeks from now we will know more about how much of my nerve and muscle response will come back. He's cautiously optimistic, but says there are no guarantees. For now, I work at physical therapy and continue to recover from what I have discovered is the very natural shock of a paralysis.

Some might wish that I would spend most of the rest of this sermon taking Jimmy Swaggart to task. And it is a temptation. We could pull out all the stops on this one. After all, much of his ministry is built on helping people define who they are as Christians at the expense of others—including Jews, Catholics, therapists, humanists and even other evangelists. I could talk about hypocrisy—his judgment of others from a position of superior holiness—all the time practicing his own version of deception. I could talk about the people who have trusted him, who have given money to support him, who are now disillusioned and adrift. (We can only hope they will find their way here, some of them, where they can find community to sustain them and an inclusive truth with which to order their lives.) I could talk about all that, but that is not my point today. My sermon is about cheap grace.

It is about tidy endings, quick-fix cures, about facile lessons and clichéd meanings and glib solutions to the deep movement of life. It is about quick forgiveness, forgiveness in the fast lane, forgiveness for a throwaway culture, a makeover culture. Forgiveness on call. Cheap grace.

But first we should talk about Grace itself. Probably one of the most quoted texts on the subject in the Christian scriptures is that in Ephesians 2:8 and 9. You former Lutherans will know it by heart. "For by grace are ye saved through faith: and that not of yourselves, it is the gift of God. Not of works, lest any man [or woman] should boast."[3]

What Paul was saying is that grace is a gift. It is life as gift. It is what comes to you beyond what you expected—often in spite of what you expected. It is most often seen in the surprise of life, in wonder, in a sudden unfolding of new life when it is least expected. It comes in the midst of our plans; changing them and letting us know, once again, that it is *not* all up to us. "For by grace are you saved through faith, and that not of yourselves. It is the Gift of God, not of works, lest any man or woman should boast."

One of the first days I was in the hospital one of the doctors came in to see me. He said, "Isn't it Methodists who believe in predestination?" "No," I answered, "it's the Presbyterians." "Oh, that's right," he replied. "That's what I am." "Unitarian Universalists believe in random events," I added.

Predestination. Does God have a plan? Does God visit us with events, with things that happen to us because He or She wants to reward us or punish us, as the case may be? Or perhaps a more Unitarian Universalist version of the question is, "Are there meanings and purposes, lessons and insights to be gained, no matter what?"

"We believe in random events," I said. I suspect there is a theology of random events somewhere. I can't remember reading about it in theological school. Perhaps in the new physics. My doctor laughed and said that made sense to him (perhaps less a Presbyterian than he thought).

I believe any discussion of Grace must begin with a theology of random events—with the belief that whatever comes from a particular event in our lives is not foreordained, predestined, calculated, meaning-laden, lesson-ripe—it just is. Whatever comes will come as the events continue to unfold, and our job is to pay attention.

It would be nice to believe that things that happen to us are personalized. That even the tragedies of our lives are shaped for us because we need them. It might redeem them, somehow. But I don't believe that. Grace, if there is grace, begins with the recognition that loss can be very real. That loss mustn't be glossed over and dressed up to look like gain. If I have one major criticism of many of the new religions of our time it is that they have a tendency to do just that—to pretend that everything that comes to us is for our gain, and it's just our job to find out how. That belief, that theology, if you will, can make us shallow. Can give us the tendency to skim off the top of experience and never move into the depths.

John Wolf, our minister in Tulsa who has taught me much of what I know about preaching, said to me several years ago that he thought the strength of my preaching was that I preached grace. That there was a thread of permission, of forgiveness, of gift that ran through my sermons that could only be described as mediating grace. I've always enjoyed that comment because it fits with much of what I believe a sermon is for. Two weeks ago he called me up and, after hearing how it was with me, asked, "How are you going to get grace out of this one?" I replied, "I'm not. At least not for awhile."

A theology of random events. One often discovers what one truly believes in a hospital bed. No grace, at least not for a while.

Now Jimmy Swaggart is *with* me on this one—at least at the beginning. He says at first he despaired of his life and prayed that God would take it. I might not have been as audacious as he—I don't presume to tell God what to do. But the spirit of what he is saying makes sense. Having built a religious structure on condemnation of others and hypocrisy of self, faced with the reality of his life, despair seems appropriate. And the actions of his governing board make sense too. (Incidentally, my colleagues in the Springfield, Missouri area—the headquarters of the Assembly of God denomination—say they are impressed with the integrity of that group. As one who sits on the equivalent board of our denomination, I admire the clarity and courage they displayed in the face of the scandal.) They said, "Don't preach for a year." Give God time. Give us time. Give yourself time to change your life and be changed by life.

Of course there were other considerations. In a year, the ministry centered around the person of Jimmy Swaggart would be most likely dissolved. There are bills to pay, after all. Whatever the reasons, Jimmy Swaggart decided he couldn't do that. And so he's back. Citing scripture, he says he has been healed of his sin, forgiven, washed by the blood of the lamb, a new person in the eyes of God.

It *could* be true. I've seen people change their lives, seemingly overnight. Make decisions, face realities, turn around. I've seen people visited by the unexpected and rise to the occasion, startling everyone around them. I've seen people experience what can only be described as grace, their experience of *life as gift* being so profound they are never the same.

But when I see someone shape events more than the events shape him; when I see someone abandoning former commitments (such as the covenant of his ordination) because new commitments better meet his purposes; then I am led to believe that God is being used, much as Jimmy Swaggart has used the people he has been ministering to, I wonder about the presence of the grace that emerges from the depths. To quote the old Alcoholic's Anonymous question, "I wonder if he's walking the talk, or if he's just talking the talk."

For my part, let me hasten to add that I have not sat for this month in the depths of despair. I am not happy each morning as I get up and remember again that a leg brace has become part of my regular wardrobe, but that is not the whole of the story. The deep caring I have felt from those of you here and from friends spread all across the continent sustained me from the very beginning. Your cards and letters were wonderful gifts to me of love and concern. The room you gave me to relinquish my public life for a time, has been a gift I have deeply appreciated.

Perhaps the first sense of life as gift in these kinds of situations comes in the midst of the beloved community, as one becomes aware of how people around us are gifts to us. There *have* been, in this month, moments of insight and understanding, moments of deep gratitude, in the midst of the shock and loss. You now have a minister who understands with fresh sensitivity all that she was taught about pastoral care. I have become keenly aware of handicapped parking places and how far it is from point A to point B at any given moment. I am grateful that our church is handicapped accessible in a way I never was before.

And one could call that grace: the grace of community, the giftedness of insight and understanding. But to be too quick to name the gifts in any given situation is, to my mind, to short circuit the process, to grasp at the apparent and leave no room for mystery. It can become, too quickly, *cheap* grace.

Paul, writing in Romans, captures in what has now become traditional language, the essence of which I speak. He says, "Hope that is seen is not hope, but the spirit helpeth our infirmities. The Spirit itself maketh intercession for us with groanings which cannot be uttered." Martin Luther, in his commentary on this passage, says, "It's not a good sign when all your prayers are answered."[4]

Grace, the gift of God/Life/the Forces among us—whatever you call it—comes in ways we can't manage, in response to prayers we can't utter, in the midst of situations where there are no guarantees. It becomes a deep existential trust that we reach, not by plan or even intention, but in recognition of that which emerges from the depths of our beings to sustain us.

How do you know if you have been visited by grace? Grace that is not cheap and expedient? When you have an overwhelming sense of gratitude, even in the midst of difficulty and pain and tragedy. When you can, at the same time, acknowledge the reality even as you are amazed at the incredible movement of life in and around you. When, as one friend said to me recently, you realize that we are all in one boat. Even Jimmy Swaggart and me. Knowing that our lives are infused with grace, in spite of our need to grasp at straws and *make* things work. By fall, I should be able to mine a lesson or two from all this. For now, I choose not to grasp at cheap grace, but to wait. Who knows what's next?

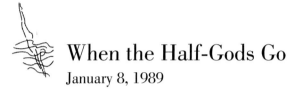

When the Half-Gods Go
January 8, 1989

This sermon is a companion to the previous one, preached six months later. It continues the story, but more than that, it sorts out grace from cheap grace with a few more startling experiences for good measure. I really did feel like Job. Or perhaps, more like Jacob—wrestling with the angel for my blessing. My half-gods of special blessing were demolished in favor of, perhaps, simply being more human. LH

.

In May of 1988 I was the victim of a bizarre medical accident in which, during a routine surgery, my left leg became paralyzed. In shock and largely disabled, I was unable to work. My appearance in June to preach was the first time back with this congregation following the surgery the month before.

At that time, I said that it was easy to jump to conclusions, to seek easy meanings and obvious purposes in things, but that I was resisting the temptation to do so. That human desire is always to have things work out for the best—and sometimes in our eagerness to do so we draw quick conclusions which are ill-founded. I was determined not to fall into that trap. If there was to be any grace in the midst of my difficulties, it would come over the long-haul, not in the immediate. I would ride it out, secretly hoping that saying the words would make it be true. For at that point I had no assurance that the feeling would return to my leg, that I would be able to walk again without assistance of a brace and crutches. I had no assurance I could continue to be your minister, a job I had held for only nine months. I had no assurance that what had happened to me would be anything but a simple tragedy which contained only loss.

Religion is full of stories of "foxhole conversions", people who find God in the midst of one crisis or another, their faith affirmed in the midst of a difficult or impossible situation. Peripheral, extraneous values are cast away and they see, as if for the first time, with clarity and purpose. Often we will hear how their lives are dramatically and instantaneously changed, and all is made new.

I did not have such an experience. Fortunately, for me, it was soon summer, and the church could more easily do without my constant presence. For it was all I could do to get through the seemingly constant sessions of physical therapy and take care of the basics of daily living. Even at that, people helped by bringing in meals, driving me places I needed to go, and doing shopping for me. In July, I was able to move my toes and began to have hope that the use of the leg would return. My brain, which had assumed that there would be no more use of that leg since it wasn't getting any messages from it, began to reclaim hope. My parents came to visit from California, eager to see how I was, and to help in any way they could. Three days after they arrived, my mother went for

21

a walk, tripped on a crack in the sidewalk, fell and shattered her hip. I began to feel at bit like Job.

It is a peculiar thing, to discover what one truly believes. I discovered, sometime during the summer, that I believed in *special blessings*. The process which had brought me to Dallas had begun, officially, almost two years before I had come. It had involved a very serious process of discernment—which meant gathering all the facts, but also meant a very deep and continuing process of searching and testing. What do I want? What do I most deeply want? Is this right and good? Do I want to give the time of *my* life to this enterprise, this endeavor? Am I willing to let go of what I have for what might be? Are there larger purposes to be served in this move?

Somehow in the midst of the process, I came to believe in the half-god of special blessings. I didn't know it at the time. It was disguised as gratitude. I tell you this because I don't believe it is only my experience, but can be part of the lives of all of us. Because of a particular constellation of events—call it luck, call it destiny, call it the will of God, call it what you may—things go well. Our effort is blessed. What we do, flourishes. And we begin to believe in special blessing. That we have a special destiny, a special path to walk. That we are unique, called out. Meaning comes to us in the work we do, in the results of our labors, even in the midst of what we give to others. God—if there be a God—comes to us in the midst of our vitality, our effort. And it is good.

But let me tell you about half-Gods. Ralph Waldo Emerson said, "Heartily know/when half-gods go/the gods arrive."[1] *Heartily* know "when half-gods go/the gods arrive."

I didn't do anything *heartily* in the summer. My mother was taken to Presbyterian Hospital in an ambulance called by some neighbors. She had emergency hip replacement surgery. In the meantime my son, who had been studying and traveling in Europe for a year, came home. After moving to Minneapolis he fell ill and was diagnosed as having tuberculosis, which doctors guess he picked up in his travels.

It is a discouraging truth that if you believe in special blessing, you are required, if the occasion calls for it, to believe in special curse. And, like Job, I began to wonder. In the process I began to understand about half-gods. These are not false gods. These are, of necessity, the gods we serve. They are the ways we get glimpses of a larger reality, but they are not the whole of the reality. And the minute we think they are, we are guilty of idolatry. It is in the moments such as I experienced in the summer we most discover the limitations of that to which we pay homage, that to which we give the time of our lives. I am a doer, and I couldn't do. I am a helper, and I was unable to help even my own mother in her distress. I am self-reliant, and I was unable to take care of the simplest chores. I am healthy, most of the time, and expect my body to be my friend, and to do whatever is required at the moment. My body was in extreme distress and rather than helping me do what was needed, needed all the help it could get. I have a sense of vitality, and was in such shock, that vitality was obscured. In short, all the ways I was in the world, and all the ways I related to the world, to life, and to events, all the elements of an I-Thou relationship, which is our essential spiritual relationship—all those ways were taken from me.

"When the half-gods go . . ." Human beings, since the beginning of time, have yearned to know God. They have had a sense that there was something beyond the temporal existence of their lives. Religion has said that what we know is but a pointer to that which is beyond, that which is mystery. We are to cherish who we are, and what we do, and how we perceive life, but always to remember that it is but a sign and a symbol of the larger mystery.

No matter what you believe about that mystery—whether it is personally interested in your existence or not, whether it has any power in this dimension in which we live or not, whether it is truly knowable or not—you would agree, I think, that life is much larger than we can know. And that from time to time, what we know is shattered in favor of something more than we can know and be. And so, whatever your belief about mystery, you can understand me when I say that this summer I lived in the midst of the shattering of half-gods. Half-gods of purpose and meaning, half-gods of self-understanding.

In June I said I would not, and could not make sense out of what had happened. That would have been "cheap" grace, I said. Since then, I have wished for a little cheap grace to come my way, because it has been hard to make any sense out of what happened. It may, in the end, have been just a simple tragedy. And finally, every faith must make room for that possibility.

In the face of the possibilities in what happened I am the first to say I am most grateful. My mother made an excellent recovery from her surgery, and my son, thanks to modern medicine, is well on the road to recovery from his illness. While I expect always to have some weakness in my leg and foot, I no longer have to use crutches or a brace to walk. I am grateful, in the face of what could have been.

Out of that gratitude comes a strange kind of amazement that most of the time we do so well. For I have realized in this time that we choose our level of denial in relation to reality. If we truly were aware of all the potential for disaster around us in every thing we did, we would be stopped in our tracks, unable to do anything. Now, of course, total denial would be as foolish, for we do have some responsibility to keep ourselves out of senseless danger. But one of the strangely comforting thoughts I had this summer is that usually what had happened to me doesn't happen. In the usual order of things, my situation was an exception.

I was comforted in the knowledge that whether I found meaning in what was happening, meaning was there. It might not be apparent. But the way I lived my life, even in this situation, did make a difference. And it was the very loss of the half-gods of health, vitality, and special blessing which made that understanding clear. I discovered I also had a half-god of insight and awareness. I found myself in a situation where I was required simply to live it, not figure it out, not discover the lessons inherent in it, not find the truth (with a capital T in it) but simply to live it.

I tell you this story today because we all live with half-gods. Mine are different from yours, although some of them may resonate with your approach to life. Over the years of our lives we come to trust certain qualities, certain ways of being. And it is right that we do so. It's the best we can do as humans.

But when the time comes that the half-gods go, for whatever reason, and we see them for what they are—simple tools for living, not ultimate sources of meaning and purpose, let us remember that even the most worthy purposes of life can cut us off from the transcendent dimension, the infinite reality we seek.

Any belief, any trust—in another person, in skills, in our commitment to bettering the world we live in, in truth, knowledge and freedom—has an element of the divine within it. Such belief and trust are essential to life itself. The only way we can know the divine is in the midst of our lived lives, as we give ourselves to that which is outside ourselves.

But when the half-gods go, for whatever reason, when a trust is broken, it is in those crucial times of doubt and even despair that we're told, "The gods arrive." We are carved out, truly enlarged, our vision is altered, our understanding changed, not through our own doing, but as part of the mystery in which we exist. From this vantage point, I have discovered this: It's not easy when the half-gods go. When one loses one's moorings, one's handhold on the way things are, it's not easy.

I do not have illusions that my vision will be clear from here on in. I suspect that other, similar half-gods will settle into my being. For, after all, as humans, that's the best we can do. But once in awhile in the last few months, I have captured a glimpse of the depth of things, small glimpses of possibility beyond insight and meaning, beyond knowledge and understanding.

To paraphrase Emerson, I would say, when the half-gods go, and before of necessity other half-gods arrive, there can be in the space between, a glimpse of grace that is grace of a different order than cheap grace. It is rare.

You will never hear me say that I am grateful for this summer's events. But I *am* grateful for having survived, for having been touched by this congregation's love in a time when I could not serve you, for regaining most of the use of my leg, and for that glimpse, however shadowed, of what lies beyond half-gods, for living that incredible paradox of life that in brokenness we become whole. May it be so for each of us.

Practice Resurrection
Easter
April 11, 1993

I have always thought of Easter as a wonderful time to 'reach deeper' into the traditional story and experience the incredible power that is inherent in it. So here I try to take away the doctrine and excessive drama that has solidified the meaning so completely that it has lost its resonance with our lives. It's time for new life to flow in our veins, and new purposes to seek us out. It's a great day. LH

Luke 24:13-53

   . . . two of them were going to a village named Emmaus, about seven miles from Jerusalem, and talking with each other about all these things that had happened.

   While they were talking and discussing together, Jesus himself drew near and went with them. But their eyes were kept from recognizing him.

   And he said to them, "What is this conversation which you are holding with each other as you walk?' And they stood still, looking sad.

   Then one of them, named Cleopas, answered him, "Are you the only visitor to Jerusalem who does not know the things that have happened there in these days?"

   And he said to them, "What things?" And they said to him, "Concerning Jesus of Nazareth, who was a prophet mighty in deed and word before God and all the people, and how our chief priests and rulers delivered him up to be condemned to death, and crucified him. But we had hoped that he was the one to redeem Israel. Yes, and besides all this, it is now the third day since this happened.

   Moreover, some women of our company amazed us. They were at the tomb early in the morning and did not find his body; and they came back saying that they had even seen a vision of angels, who said that he was alive. Some of those who were with us went to the tomb, and found it just as the women had said; but him they did not see."

   They drew near to the village to which they were going. He appeared to be going further, but they constrained him, saying, "Stay with us, for it is toward evening and the day is now far spent." So he went in to stay with them. When he was at table with them, he took the bread and blessed, and broke it, and gave it to them. And their eyes were opened and they recognized him; and he vanished out of their sight. They said to each other, "Did not our hearts burn within us while he talked to us on the road . . ."

An excerpt from *Manifesto: The Mad Farmer Liberation Front*
By Wendell Berry

> Go with your love to the fields.
> Lie down in the shade. Rest your head
> in her lap. Swear allegiance
> to what is nighest your thoughts.
>
> As soon as the generals and the politicos
> can predict the motions of your mind,
> lose it. Leave it as a sign
> to mark the false trail, the way
> you didn't go.
>
> Be like the fox
> who makes more tracks than necessary,
> some in the wrong direction.
> Practice resurrection.[1]

It would be a big mistake to spend the morning explaining away the resurrection story. To analyze the text. To speak against the miraculous nature of the account. It would also be a mistake to ignore it today. To pretend that the Christian story of Jesus' resurrection has nothing to do with the lives we live today, at the end of the 20th century.

You did not come today because a myth needs debunking, or because it is a day just like any other day. It may not be clear to you why you are here today. For some it is a habit, this hour of solitude and quiet, of word and song. You are here as part of a regular spiritual and communal practice for your life. But others of you have come perhaps for the first time. The impulse to come to church on this day having arisen, you decided to join us (rather than a more traditional Christian church) on this Easter holy day. However that may be, it is this impulse toward the spiritual, this impulse toward the communal in this season of resurrection, whether long-standing or new, that I want to speak to today.

Now, for a moment I must talk about the story. For there are at least three versions of Jesus in the Easter story. It helps to meet them all.

First there is the story of the very human events around the death of Jesus. He died. His death was a profound moment of political buck-passing and appeasement, personal abandonment, and denial—as well as a tragic moment of suffering and pain. It was all any of us have experienced of death around us. That's one Jesus: the very human man who suffered and died.

Another is the story of Jesus as a Messiah who came to redeem humankind. Each event of his life and death is tied to a prophecy, to a rational construct of history that includes the redemption of us all. The Jesus in this text often lives outside time and humanity.

The third Jesus is the made-for-TV/movie-Jesus. He is still quite human, but the events are exaggerated, are forged in a story, which has just enough that is miraculous, just enough literary tension that it keeps our attention and focuses our vision. It is the Metro/Goldwyn/Meyer School of storytelling, with the events writ large, so that we don't miss the point.

It is easier to sort out the story, to see its depth, with these three portrayals of Jesus in mind: the very human story of Jesus' betrayal and abandonment, the Messianic story of the historic purposes and prophetic fulfillment of his life, and the made-for-TV story with certain elements exaggerated to make a dramatic point. If we are to practice resurrection, as I will suggest today, we'd better know which resurrection we're practicing.

This kind of resurrection, I will suggest, has to do with the first portrayal, in which Jesus embodies the gift of hope and purpose in the face of death and despair. This is a very human story.

Now, I will admit, there are some great made-for-TV moments. The Road to Emmaus story is one of them. Two men are walking along, talking, and a third joins them. They don't recognize him, even though we know who he is. They are astounded that he doesn't know what has happened. Then they explain (this is a Messianic paragraph): "We hoped he was the one who was to redeem Israel. And now it is three days since he died."

The made-for-TV part of the story sets us up. We say to ourselves, "The third day. They don't know yet that he will rise on the third day. They're disappointed now, but they won't be for long." That's our unwritten, but implied part that leads us into the Messianic conclusion—he's there to fulfill prophecy, to complete history. We're lured in.

But if we read the story with these three threads in mind, it will become clear. When Jesus asks them what they are talking about, they stand still, looking sad. Very human. They talk some more. The tomb is empty, they say (Messianic story). They offer him hospitality (Human story).

If it is possible for us to practice resurrection, as I will suggest today, then we must look to the human elements of the story, whether they are related directly (we are told the men are sad) or pointed to dramatically (the moment they saw him, he disappeared). If we are to practice resurrection, then we must look at what the story tells us about being *human*. For that is our task: practicing resurrection in the midst of being human.

The resurrection story could be considered epilogue, an ending, an addition, after the main story is told. The resurrection story could be an epilogue but not so much about Jesus, as it is about the disciples.

In the Messianic story, the disciples are in despair, in disarray—confused and trying to reclaim their lives. There are intimations that something else is about to occur, but the men on the road to Emmaeus are sad and speechless when asked what has happened.

In the "Made-for-TV" story, the disciples are in despair, confused, etc. The hope for a King is gone. The personal love and wisdom and power of the teacher Jesus is gone. They are overcome by death, and are back to their fishing, their work, and their lives—with much grief and little hope. Emptiness—empty tomb, empty future, empty lives, is what they know.

But in the human story, on the road to Emmaeus, they don't recognize him, but later they remember that their hearts burned within them on the road. They realize that while he is gone, much remains. There is a spiritual presence.

We can know that. Beyond the loss, there is a presence, after one is gone. We can know that. Our hearts burned within us, remember? Recognize resurrection. Notice when your heart tells you love remains.

He appears to some fishermen who haven't caught anything all night. "Fish on the other side of the boat," he says. Practice resurrection. Fish on the other side of the boat. There's nothing on this side left. Try the other side. Practice resurrection by looking around, seeing something else, throwing your line on the other side. Jesus appears and disappears here and there, in various places and ways.

Though the Christian church has turned this fantastic story into doctrine and dogma, wringing out every droplet of the dynamic, mysterious truth it is pointing to, still we can imagine the screenwriter wondering how to portray what was human, what was real. "A montage," we can imagine him or her thinking, "of presence and absence. By juxtaposing the presence and absence of Jesus after his death, I can suggest that he was gone, and yet with them."

Whatever the dramatic flourishes, the reality of the very human story is that the disciples went from absolute despair and fragmentation, to go on to establish a faith which was to capture the imagination and loyalty of large portions of the world's population. Whatever the dramatic flourishes, the reality of this story is that something happened to them. Something unexpected, something more miraculous than any flight through the sky to a home above. More miraculous than anybody could imagine. For after the death of the person they had given their lives to, the death of someone they deeply loved, the death of someone they thought would save them, the miracle is that they were galvanized into writing, into teaching, into talking, into being together again. They had each gone their separate ways, but they were galvanized into a community that began to embody the very things he had taught.

Now, they did it in a flawed way. It *is* a human story, after all. Not everything they did was full of love and truth. But as far as we can see, they did the best they could, in their time and place. Jesus' teachings, his very life, were shared with all who would hear.

The stories of love and inclusiveness were taught. We're still, to this day, insufficiently living the teachings of Jesus, but he and those who followed him set the course for those of us who care. Care about the poor. Share what you have. Love one another, even your enemies. Know that God loves you.

Simple teachings that died and then came alive again. A presence that was lost and then regained. A power that could not save him from the cross—reemerged.

I believe that such deaths find their resurrection in us, only as much as we can realize it. Gandhi's life, lost to us, lived on in Martin Luther King and Thomas Merton, to name only two. Martin Luther King and Thomas Merton's power and wisdom live on in us, as we pay attention to their truth.

Practicing resurrection is tricky. Because it implies that we can raise the dead ourselves, if not literally, then spiritually. But practicing resurrection, at least as I see it taught by great teachers is more a process of participation, than playing God.

We can hone our skills of observation. We can practice looking, feeling, seeing, loving. We can practice paying attention, so when the word to fish on the other side of the boat comes, we won't miss it. When our hearts burn, we will feel it. When the stranger comes, we will welcome him or her. When the future opens before us, we will step into it. Practicing resurrection is like practicing the piano. It takes discipline, it takes time, it takes regular attention. And then when the miracle of the music comes, we are ready.

Today, as one of my colleagues suggests, we "practice the scales of rejoicing," rejoicing that we are alive, that we are together. That power and meaning are all around us. And love. And while we don't know what's coming, especially for our own individual lives, we do know that truth and love and hope abide with us, and are continued through and beyond us.

I think the writers of the gospels are part of Wendell Berry. When the gospel writers talk about Jesus' appearances and disappearances, Wendell Berry replies, "Do something every day that doesn't compute." When the gospel writers say Jesus taught us to "Fish on the other side of the boat", Wendell Berry replies, "Swear allegiance to what is nighest your thoughts." When they write that Jesus rose again, Wendell Berry replies, "Put your ear close, and hear the faint chattering of the songs that are to come." When they say, "And the disciples went forth and preached everywhere", Wendell Berry replies, "Practice Resurrection."

Like A Pool into Which We Plunge, or Do Not Plunge

March 19, 1995

This sermon was preached at the Sunday worship service at the Unitarian Universalist Ministers' Convocation in Little Rock, Arkansas. The theme of the conference was "The Transient and Permanent in Unitarian Universalism". Our goal for our time together was to create a covenant that would embody our commitment to each other, the holy, and our larger work. LH

Reading

From the sermon preached by John Winthrop, the first leader of the Massachusetts Bay Colony, on board ship in 1630, before stepping foot on what for them was the New World.

Thus stands the cause between God and us. We are entered into Covenant with him for this work, we have taken out a Commission, the Lord hath given us leave to draw our own Articles, we have professed to enterprise these Actions upon these and these ends, we have hereupon besought him of favor and blessing: Now if the Lord shall please to hear us, and bring us in peace to the place we desire, then hath he ratified this Covenant and sealed our Commission and will expect a strict performance of the Articles contained in it. But if we shall neglect the observation of these Articles which are the ends we have propounded, and dissembl(e) with our God . . . the Lord will surely break out in wrath against us, be revenged of such a perjured people and make us know the price of the breach of such a Covenant.

Now the only way to avoid this shipwreck and to provide for our posterity is to follow the Council of Micah, to do Justly, to love mercy, to walk humbly with our God. For this end, we must be knit together in this work as one man, we must entertain each other in brotherly Affection, we must be willing to abridge ourselves of our superfluities, for the supply of others necessities, we must uphold a familiar Commerce together in all meekness, gentleness, patience and liberality, we must delight in each other, make others Conditions our own, rejoice together, mourn together, labor and suffer together, always having before our eyes our Commission and Community in the work. Therefore let us choose life, that we, and our seed, may live: by obeying his voice, and cleaving to him, for he is our life, and our prosperity.[1]

There Are No Gods
By D.H. Lawrence

> There are no gods, and you can please yourself
> have a game of tennis, go out in the car, do some shopping, sit and
>   talk, talk, talk,
> with a cigarette browning in your fingers.
>
> There are no gods, and you can please yourself—
> go and please yourself—
>
> But leave me alone, leave me alone, to myself!
> and then in the room, whose is the presence
> that makes the air so still and lovely to me?
>
> Who is it that softly touches the sides of my breast
> and touches me over the heart
> so that my heart beats soothed, soothed, soothed and at peace?
>
> Who is it smooths the bed-sheets like the cool
> smooth ocean when the fishes rest on edge
> in their own dream?
>
> Who is it that clasps and kneads my naked feet, till they unfold,
> till all is well, till all is utterly well? the lotus-lilies of the feet!
>
> I tell you, it is no woman, it is no man, for I am alone.
> And I fall asleep with the gods, the gods
> that are not, or that are
> according to the soul's desire,
> like a pool into which we plunge, or do not plunge.[2]

As I struggled with the relationship of our stated covenant to our felt commitment, D.H. Lawrence's poem came to me: "Go and please yourself," "Leave me alone to myself," he says. "There are no Gods . . . Talk, talk, talk . . . Play . . . Do . . . Leave me alone."

This poem is a remarkably accurate description of contemporary life. (Postmodern contemporary life, I would venture to say.) One without illusion—there are no gods, after all—where we find ourselves busy with the tasks of our lives, running errands, doing a little shopping.

These days we'd most likely leave out the cigarette browning in the fingers, but some would say that sitting and talking, talking, talking could be the primary spiritual practice of our faith. Even playing tennis can't be faulted. After all, we need to keep in shape to keep our blood pressure down and our stress in check. I don't know about you, but I even resonate with the part about being left alone. After a long day at church, the idea of saying, "Go and please yourself, just leave me alone to myself'" does have a certain ring to it!

This poetic picture painted by Lawrence came to me as a good description of our lives. For, if there is anything necessary for us to pledge *to one another*, it is against the backdrop of our struggles to do the small tasks of ministry, to keep ourselves healthy, to talk things through and not be deluded by fantasies. It is against the backdrop of the urge to withdraw from the relentless demands of life and be left alone. It is even against the urge to withhold our deepest selves from this covenanting process. To stand back, if only internally, from the commitments we are asked to make.

"But then," against the backdrop of those activities and our reticence, Lawrence asks, "But then in the room, whose is that presence . . ." *"Whose is that presence?"* is *the* covenantal question. "Whose is that presence" is the essential question of sacred relationship. My friend and colleague Harry Scholefield calls it the "You" of life. Theologian Martin Buber called it the relationship with the "Thou" of life. Religious Historian Mircea Eliade named it "The Other." But whatever our names, and there are many, there is an essential "You" of life with which we are constantly and dynamically related. Lawrence says, it is "like a pool into which we plunge, or do not plunge." Today I want to say that—beyond our words, or even our intentions—our covenant is "like a pool into which we plunge, or do not plunge." It is entered into by plunging, by jumping off, by diving.

There is, in Dallas, a young woman named Cheril Santini. A senior at Southern Methodist University, she has been a member of the National Diving Team for the last three years and is in training for the 1996 Olympics. This week she is participating in the NCAA Diving Competition in the hope of securing a position on the Olympic team. After reading about her in the paper, I decided to call her up to find out what it is like to dive.

She said, "When you dive, you're always afraid. You don't know how you're going to land, so there's always the fear. But the fear is important, because it helps you focus. You want to have enough fear to help you concentrate."

It is obvious, of course, that there would be fear before doing a high dive. Natural, organic, visceral fear in response to the plan to fling one's body off a board into empty air. That fear could be helpful is something we might do well to consider. We who soothe brows, who comfort, who facilitate communication among and between people and groups—alleviating anxiety and fear whenever we can—might find wisdom in thinking about the role anxiety plays in focusing attention, in signaling the importance of the commitment at hand, in telling us we are about to dive.

"Sometimes," she said, "my mind starts to race and I start thinking . . . . what if? What if I come too close to the board and hit it? What if I forget how to do the dive? I start second-guessing myself. My coach tells me that when fear starts to paralyze me it is usually because I am indulging in over-analysis. I have to learn to think of the whole and let my body dive."

Think about the whole and let ourselves dive . . . It's not easy, this keeping the larger vision when we are writing the poetry we need for our covenant. It is not easy, once written, to let ourselves dive.

Cheril and I talked a little more about her future, about pride and possibilities, about each dive being the only one. I uttered a little prayer of gratitude that I had found a verbal diver, and we hung up. Keep your eye on the papers; Cheril Santini may be plunging into Olympic Pools before long.

Incidentally, at the end of our conversation, she said "Good luck with your sermon." I thought, *she's* the one going to the Olympics! But her good wishes made me realize that I *do* dive. *We* dive. Perhaps one of our longest dives was into Ordination. But there are many dives in the ministry. We know about fear. We know about over analysis. We even know about each courageous act being the only one.

As I imagined Cheril standing on a high board, slightly afraid, focused, taking those steps forward that would propel her off the board and into the dive, I imagined us. Perhaps not as sinewy. Not as toned. But we know what we can do. We too can paralyze ourselves with over analysis. And, like Cheril, we don't know how it will come out.

I am reminded of the story of Moses at the Red Sea. Standing before the water with the Egyptian soldiers pressing in, Moses lifted his staff to part the waters and nothing happened. Anxiety rising, the crowd pressing against him as there was nowhere else to go, he took a step into the water and the sea parted. Not until the step was taken did the miracle occur. Not until the first step is taken on the high board, does the dive begin. Not until we commit, is the covenant real. Our covenant begins with the words of our agreement, but it is fulfilled in the step, the plunge into the pool.

Cheril said, "You have to put all your muscle into the water. If you work *with* the water, it will be beautiful." That is one of the most succinct statements of the I-You, or I-Thou relationship I have ever heard. Cheril has a very clear understanding of who she is and what she can do in relationship to the water. The boundaries are not blurred. The dive for her is an affirmation of her power, her place, and her ability. At the same time, she knows where the water begins, and its potentially harsh judgment of her dive.

Even with all Cheril can suggest that helps us understand our dive, there are limits to her ability to help us. She's on a team, she does not dive in isolation. We're not taking turns on the high board, we are diving together. Cheril is diving into a clear chlorinated pool. We're flinging ourselves into a cloudy future, into the varied waters of the future—calm and turbulent, shallow and deep, nurturing and frightening, requiring responses we might not even imagine. Diving into the pool, putting all our muscle (everything we know and are) into the water, we have no assurance that—even with our combined experience and wisdom, our noble tradition and committed energy—our plunge will be as we hope. For we are plunging, as best we can, into the mystery, into the unknown—headlong into the 'you' of life, into 'the other.'

This is, of course, what John Winthrop knew on board his ship in 1630. It was a different time and place, and for him, the 'other' of life was clearly named. It was God. The dive was clearly marked. If they dissembled, he said, if they were confused about their intention, or the demands of what they were about to do, the Lord would make them know the price of the breach of the covenant.

"The only way to avoid a shipwreck and provide for posterity," Winthrop said, "Would be to follow the Council of Micah 'to do justly, to love mercy, and to walk humbly with our God. We must knit together in this work as one people, we must be willing to abridge ourselves of our superfluities, we must delight in each other, make others' conditions our own, rejoice together, mourn together, labor and suffer together, always having before our eyes our Commission and Community in the work . . .'"

This is a plunge, a dive, of a different order than the heroic half gainer with a triple twist from the high board. This is a constant and dedicated effort to embody the spirit of meekness, gentleness, patience, liberality and delight among ourselves, in the service of a larger work.

If our covenant included the qualities of spirit we yearn to have with one another as we do the work (they might not be the same as Winthrop's, but it's not a bad place to start) and it included our commission in time and history, it would be sufficient.

If it included the larger demands of God which John Winthrop understood so keenly (it would not necessarily have the same judgment and spirit as Winthrop's, but again, we might want to start there) it would be real.

Because John Winthrop was right. His worry was that the eager shipboard congregation would forget their intentions and their calling. They would forget humility and mercy. They would forget justice. Their contentiousness would break them apart. They would dissemble and seek only their own goals. To avoid that shipwreck they were to follow the Council of Micah, he said. To avoid shipwreck they were to do justly, to love mercy, and to walk humbly with their God.

With the benefit of hindsight—hindsight always making us feel wise—we can see that Winthrop could not possibly have known what justice, mercy and humility would have required. He could not have known that his vision of God was too narrow, that even his vision of their purpose and mission was blind to many realities. But—whether by failure of their vision of God or failure of their perception of mission, or failure of the will of the people—we (and Winthrop) would say that the shipwreck he feared has occurred.

Adrienne Rich's poem, *Diving into the Wreck,* seems to have been written as a response to Winthrop. In it she goes down into the ocean as a deep sea diver. She says, if we dive, it will be into the wreck.

> I came to explore the
> wreck. The words are
> purposes.
> The words are maps.
> I came to see the damage
> that was done and the
> treasures that prevail.[3]

I imagine that none of us thought our words of covenant were maps and purposes for diving into a wreck. But perhaps that is a place to begin. Rich says that the wreck is a wreck of our *perceptions.* She says, by cowardice or courage, we are the ones who find our way back to the scene of the wreck.

If our covenant includes the qualities of spirit we yearn to have with one another as we do the work, as well as our commission in time and history, it would be sufficient. If it includes the larger demands of God, which John Winthrop understood so keenly, it will be real. Because, facing those demands, in whatever language or era they were forged, pulls us into the wreck of the intentions and covenants that have gone before. We have to swim into that wreck.

Rich says, "We circle silently about the wreck, we dive into the hold." Today, in relation to our covenanting together, I would suggest that diving into the wreck (she says the wreck itself, and not the story of the wreck) is where we should begin. Not in despair. But in a clear understanding of what it is we are doing.

For the treasures which we cherish—the treasures which endure and which we seek to embody in our covenant—always abide within the wreck of transient vows, limited experience of God and limited names for God, as well as limited perceptions of the time and its demands. Always. If we cannot forgive these limitations of our religious ancestors, we will not be able to claim the treasure that exists within our own finitude. If our covenant is only a heroic *verbal* high dive, only an agreement among and between us, we will remain in the shallows. If we cannot dive into the wreck, acknowledging the elements of transience in all covenants, we will not be able to claim the treasure that has endured, and will endure.

The God of Winthrop may not be our God. The wreck of Adrienne Rich may not be our wreck. But if we dare to take a plunge into the depths, there are gods and wrecks we can recognize as our own. If we dare to take such a plunge as we covenant here together, then we will know what is real, what is permanent and endures and what is transient and rusts away.

Who *we are* then, becomes the first essential question as we covenant together. Where our disciplines have brought us. What our religious ancestors have given us. How we can be true to the spirit of who we are in our strengths and limitations.

The second question is how we know and experience the gods we serve and the names we give that knowing, the You Are. This is the naming of our dynamic relationship with the You, the presence, the Sacred Other of life, and the naming of all that that relationship requires.

The third is our deepest yearnings. We covenant together knowing we are diving into the wreck, and yet also knowing that is where our enduring treasure is to be found. Being guided by our yearnings and by our fearsome commitments.

The words of covenant we craft are purposes, they are maps to the depths, to the treasure. But, what matters most is that we plunge into the depths *together*, in faithfulness and in hope. That we live in the spirit of those who have forged covenants—be they wandering nomads in the wilderness, pilgrims poised on a new land, writers of affirmations and covenants gone by—Unitarian Universalist ministers struggling, as we are, with words and actions that give shape and form to the dynamic relationship with what is and could be. That we live—in their spirit of fierce love, devoted freedom, fearless truth, and civil contentiousness—with one another, and with God.

What matters is that some distant day, when we are gone and other swimmers and divers come along—swimming among the wreck of our desire and intentions, finding the rust and weathered instruments of our covenant—that they find not only the hulk of a wreck, but also find the treasure that shines in grace and glory. That they find that which endures beyond time because we have carried it forward in the spirit of our covenanted living of our lives and our faith, together. That they find names for their Gods which can endure; names for their yearnings and hopes which can give life; names for the We Are and You Are they experience; names for the yearning, mercy and justice that is needed for their time because our covenant, our treasure, our hope, our love, our freedom endures. That is what matters.

It Has Made All the Difference
August 20, 1995

Like everyone else, ministers go through tough times. This sermon looked back on events in my life that were distant enough that I could speak of the context within which I had lived them. The context was my life in the Unitarian Universalist church that was not just a lifestyle choice but, especially in difficult times, a place that took the difficult events and gave me a context of depth within which to live. LH

Reading

Excerpt from "All Beliefs"
By David Rankin

I abandoned the church (of my childhood) for nine years. I joked about religion with my sophisticated friends. I joined the religious experts of the cocktail circuit. After all, I was young, and educated, and independent. Who needs the church? Who needs religion? I could develop my own beliefs without the discipline of an institution.

But then, the odyssey of return. It was a slow and difficult process, with no logical progression.

Out of the emptiness and despair of the secular world;
Out of the hunger and the thirst for the meaning of life;
Out of the weariness and the boredom of daily routine;
Out of the desire and the need to relate to community
Out of the wonder and mystery of my own existence;
I returned to a religious community . . . .

In many ways the Unitarian Univeralists are similar to other religions.

Like the Roman Catholics, we have a long tradition—extending back to the sun-baked desert of ancient Israel, the small rural villages of Transylvania, and the rocky shores of early New England.

Like the Jews, we have our heroes and heroines—Servetus, David, and Fuller; Murray, Channing, and Emerson; Barton, Anthony, and Steinmetz—to name only a few.

Like the Baptists, we have a system of democratic polity—with the congregation as the ultimate authority, an elected Board of Trustees, and a pulpit characterized by freedom of expression.

Like the Confucianists, we have emphasized the capacity for reason—possessing a thirst for the fruits of wisdom and knowledge, and a reverent feeling toward the achievements of the mind.

Like the Hindus, we have an eclectic system of theology—encouraging each individual to develop a personal faith which is not dependent on external demand.

Like the Humanists, we have our roots in the experience of the world—it is known through the medium of touch, and sight, and taste and smell.

Like the Buddhists, we have an accent on . . . the beauty, the mystery, and the holiness of each man, woman, and child—as each is a sacred vessel.

. . . . Finally, a personal word. The return to organized religion has been one of the most significant events of my life. In the Unitarian Universalist faith, I have found a religion which suits my needs and temperament; which offers joy and hope in daily living; which provides an impetus for ethical commitment; which encourages a community of love and trust. It is good to have a religious home.

Fortunately, I am also able to look back on the small Methodist church of my youth with a positive feeling of gratitude. The people were tender and kind. The ministers were earnest and dedicated. The church was warm and friendly. Even the Apostles' Creed, seen from a new perspective, has elements which are interesting and penetrating. (It is good to see it all as essential to who I am.)[1]

From *The Wind in Both Ears*
By Angus MacLean

(MacLean was born in Nova Scotia in 1892 and reared a Presbyterian. He became a strong voice as a Universalist teacher and minister. He writes in the third person in the style of his time, but it is his story.)

There were many factors that came from his Presbyterian faith that made a great difference in his life.

First, his faith took life very seriously. How one thought and felt and behaved made a great deal of difference, in cosmic as well as in personal terms. The all-seeing eye of God could not easily be put off the scent of the sinner. So, no matter how rebellious our young friend became he could never cease to be religious. Were he destined to be agnostic he was also destined to be devotedly and religiously atheistic. The Presbyterian cosmos was interested in him, and even though he lost his faith he could never lose a passionate interest in the cosmos as one involved in it. So no blossom could break the sod in spring without stirring mind and heart to dialogue and devotion.

Life could not be trifled with, and it was compellingly interesting. Life demanded respect, and it was insistent in its demand to be understood. Life's joys could be heartily shared but in the knowledge that life could hurt deeply, that it summoned to great enterprise, and that (our) response made all the difference.

The faith also spoke of God the good and the devil of evil at eternal war with each other. Both might be discredited (as they were) but the sense of right and wrong remained, along with the ever urgent need to differentiate between the true and the false, between the pretense and the reality of motive, between the genuine and the counterfeit . . . .

This young man's faith provided him with his basic value structure, and with values that helped make this structure operative. So if today he cannot snitch your property, this is why. If he cannot equivocate and evade, this is why. If he doesn't commit adultery or play the horses or borrow what he cannot hope to repay, or is in no danger of knocking your block off no matter how much he feels like it, this is why. If his word is as good as his bond, this is why. If he is one of those you would not need to fear even if there wasn't a law or police in the land, this is why. If he doesn't lay up treasures for the moth or the rust, this is why. If he persists in dreams of good things for humanity, this is why . . . .

I suspect that, as I have said, we came out of orthodoxy, at least in part, . . . because of valuable contributions from that orthodoxy. I think it important to make this point because I believe that to be really and constructively free, one has to make one's peace with one's cultural background, be it good or bad—a peace made up of some appreciation, some understanding, some forgiveness. We do this in retrospect for our parents when we outgrow adolescent rebellion, and we must do so with our cradle cultures . . . .

So if we have found a faith that commands us, some of us at least can say "thanks" to the folks who created difficulties for us and loved us too, probably, but whose spiritual home could not be ours.[2]

When I was in theological school, I was taught that a minister should tell his or her 'story', his or her 'spiritual odyssey', once a year. It is important, I was told, that people know the context of a minister's preaching—the life events that shape the preacher's words each Sunday.

Wary of too much self-indulgence—but also aware that in some large way, everything I say from this pulpit is part of my story—I have found this to be good advice, all the same. And while I don't know that I've made a point of doing it every year, it seemed it might be time now to revisit that story with its theological and spiritual dimensions, so you know who is preaching and ministering to you. I also tell it, acknowledging the possibility that it will resonate with some of your own journeys.

As soon as I began to think about what I would say today, words I heard many years ago came to me. It was at a General Assembly, our annual continent-wide denominational conference. Gene Pickett was speaking—most likely at the end of his time as President of our Denomination—about his journey, and saying that the Unitarian Universalist Church was primary to his life. "It has made all the difference," he said.

When I began to think about what I would say today, his words planted themselves in front of me: "It has made all the difference." Because it has. Now you might say, "Of course it has. It is your job, your career, your calling, your commitment." One could say that about anything that occupied him or her as much as the Unitarian Universalist church has occupied me. But today I hope to speak in a more personal sense. I want to speak of our church and our way in religion for me as a person seeking, hoping, trying to work things out in the midst of the demands and challenges of life.

I was raised a Conservative Baptist in San Francisco, California, which is somewhat of an oxymoron in and of itself. That wonderfully pluralistic city—even in the 1940s and '50s—shaped my perceptions and understandings as much as did my close, loving, judgmental, literalist church. My great grandfather had been a circuit-riding "Hard-shell" Baptist minister in Kansas. My grandmother was a strict and overwhelming religious presence. I remember her once discovering me knitting on a Sunday, and then quoting scriptures against work on Sunday until I stopped. My parents were not as strict. My father attended church occasionally and, I now know, leavened the strictness of the church for me by his distance. But, week after week, at Calvary Baptist Church of San Francisco—where we thought Billy Graham was too liberal—I learned of the love of Jesus and the judgment of God. An interesting combination.

Perhaps it was my disposition and inclination—perhaps it was natural given my environment—but I decided to devote myself to God very early on. I decided to become a missionary. That decision in fourth grade was softened somewhat in high school. But still, as probably one of the first young people to try to be popular for Jesus, I was Student Body Vice President, President of the Pep Club, carried my Bible on the top of my books, didn't dance—we had alternative functions at the church—or do much else that was 'worldly'. I learned to witness in church at Wednesday night prayer meetings. It was great preparation for public speaking. I led the choir when it was needed.

If I were to say what the most significant turn in my life has been, it was probably when I decided where I would go to college. Education was very important in our family. My mother and aunt had been teachers, my older brother, whom I adored, had gone to Stanford. I decided to go to Westmont Bible College and study to be a teacher. I went on a prospective student visit with my parents the spring I was to graduate, and on the way home told them I didn't want to go there. I didn't know why, but it just didn't seem right. Though I didn't know it then, it was the beginning.

I enrolled in a state university and was an active Baptist for three more years before I left that church with several of my friends and became a Quaker. I have said this before in this context, but it is important to say it here. I never underestimate the significance of a person's move into or out of a church. In our culture, we have come to think of this as a 'lifestyle change'. Move cities and change churches—perhaps to a new denomination—choosing among all the possible preachers or Sunday Schools in town. Perhaps for adults it can be just that, picking a church within a certain range of possibilities. But for me at that time, it was a monumental shift. I had no idea how much it would affect me. Because when a person has been reared in a religious system as closed as mine, leaving the church means leaving everything; when one part of it goes, the whole thing goes.

I found myself at the end of my college years without mooring, without an anchor. It was, as spiritual teachers have said, a "dark night of the soul." Life went on, of course. I graduated, found a job teaching and married. My husband, whom I had met at my church when I was 15, had become in the intervening years a student at the University of Minnesota and a Unitarian Universalist.

Soon after I moved to Minnesota, he took me to the Unitarian Universalist Church in St. Paul. Arthur Foote was preaching. Son of a Quaker mother and a Unitarian Minister father, he was the perfect minister for me to meet. He was a man of integrity, intelligence, social commitment and spiritual depth—a quiet and serene spirit who preached to my heart, soul and mind every Sunday. I wouldn't miss a week.

One day Rev. Foote asked me what the religion of my family was. When I said "Baptist" he replied, "Oh, then you have a wonderful sense of our independence. We share that with the Baptists—organizing each church independently and believing there is no intermediary between a person and God." I expect he did not have any idea of the gift he gave me that day, casting a line from my present life back to my past life. When I found out that Emerson had been a Unitarian minister, I felt even more connected. Thoreau, too, had been a source of great inspiration when I was in high school, and his connection with the Unitarians was a great joy to me.

Those were not easy years in the icy tundra of the north. Teaching school was not easy and my marriage was never strong. The church became a kind of refuge of friendship and nourishment for me, even though I only attended on Sunday for the first five years I was there. Arthur Foote retired and Roy Phillips became the minister. I've spoken recently of the years I worked on the Religious Education curriculum in that church and the impact it had on me. But, perhaps the most important moment in my spiritual development as a Unitarian Universalist—for by that time I had become stronger and more independent and more objectively interested in religion—was the day I asked Roy Phillips, as nonchalantly as I could, if he prayed. "Yes" he said. That "yes" opened up a new world: religion could be an open journey, an experiment with the "yes" of life, and all the other names we might give life as it comes to us. Prayer, I discovered, had less to do with who God is, than who I was, and what my yearnings were. Like any relationship I had, I could not define the other, only myself as I was in it.

There are of course, many other events in my life that have shaped me. One is that my son, who was born in 1970, was diagnosed with Tourette syndrome in 1981. This is a neurological disorder that affects people (mostly children) with ticks, inadvertent vocal sounds and obsessions. Peter was one of the lucky ones; in late adolescence he largely 'grew out of it' as his cerebral cortex matured.

But it was in the context of the church that he was accepted. It was in the church that we were supported and loved. In an incredible turn/grace/paradox of life, as he has grown older, his obsession with sound turned into a gift for music and language. His need to be aware of his surroundings, in case he would have to leave a group, has led to a tender awareness of people and an astute ability to observe what is going on beyond the surface of things.

It helped me keep in suspension my first judgments about situations. To wait until I have more information before rushing in to judge or even to help. It helped me realize that the lives of children and their parents are complex, and not always easily understood. Living those nine years between the time he began to show symptoms and the time he was diagnosed, I know what it is like to keep swimming when there is no shore in sight, when you have no sense of what is, or what could be. That experience has taught me about tenacity. It has taught me about the spiritual practice of discernment—of knowing that goes much deeper than body language, than psychological understanding, or the apparent facts of a situation. The church was there to give me what I needed when I needed it: friendship, comfort, weekly markers of worship. A place to bring my life and find the stories, practices, rituals and people who could inspire and teach me as I was, and help me become the person I would be.

I came to believe, over time, and in church, that events are laden with meaning, but only as we live them, not as we try to decipher them. It is the difference between speculative theology, which seeks to find and name the structure of things (which has its place, but not usually in events of this sort), and living one's relationship with Life. I learned a lot about loss, and grief, and anger, and . . . gratitude (though *that* didn't come for a long time).

It's rather terrifying to realize that there is no protective shell around us. A shell—created because we're special, or good, or do spiritual practice, or love God, or for all the reasons that we know and don't know we have—for protecting ourselves from all that we fear. I am now, most of the time, just grateful to be, here, in this life, in this place, even with all its difficulties and terrors, and to be liberated from the need to live protectively.

I'm not sure what these varied events and challenges and turns would have meant if I had lived them outside the church. I am certain that there would have been other sources of help and nourishment, inspiration and comfort. But this faith, this church, and the other Unitarian Universalist churches I have known have contributed significantly to my ability to live my life deeply as it has unfolded. Internal changes becoming, not threats to faith, but invitations to move on in different ways. That, of course, is not all of it. But, as it was for Angus MacLean and David Rankin, from my very earliest memories to this day, my Unitarian Universalist faith is here with me—enriching me, challenging me, and giving voice to my deepest yearnings.

My story is not any more startling or unusual than the stories of many of you here: triumphs and losses, meaning and loss of meaning. But here, in this place, in this church and others like it, I can say, "It has made all the difference." May it be so for you.

The Good Marriage
February 11, 1996

This began as a silly verbal exercise with a friend, and ended as a definite favorite of the members of my congregation. I've often thought it should be in print. So here it is! LH

Reading
The Gift of Love
I Corinthians 13

If I speak in the tongues of mortals and of angels, but do not have love, I am a noisy gong or a clanging cymbal. And if I have prophetic powers, and understand all mysteries and all knowledge, and if I have all faith, so as to remove mountains, but do not have love, I am nothing. If I give away all my possessions, and if I hand over my body so that I may boast, but do not have love, I gain nothing.

Love is patient; love is kind; love is not envious or boastful or arrogant or rude. It does not insist on its own way; it is not irritable or resentful; it does not rejoice in wrongdoing, but rejoices in the truth. It bears all things, believes all things, hopes all things, endures all things.

Love never ends. But as for prophecies, they will come to an end; as for tongues, they will cease; as for knowledge, it will come to an end. For we know only in part, and we prophesy only in part; but when the complete comes, the partial will come to an end. When I was a child, I spoke like a child, I thought like a child, I reasoned like a child; when I became an adult, I put an end to childish ways. For now we see in a mirror, dimly, but then we will see face to face. Now I know only in part; then I will know fully, even as I have been fully known. And now faith, hope, and love abide, these three; and the greatest of these is love.

I know that about 50% of you are married. That includes those of you who are in life-long commitments, as they say, 'with benefit of clergy'—including several gay and lesbian couples whose Services of Union we and others have witnessed.

While today I am speaking of marriage as a very specific state of being for many, but not all of us, I want to remind all of us, single and committed, that the spiritual tasks of being single and being married are very similar. And, I would add that the health of the marriages in our culture has a significant impact on the health of all of us. Whether married or not, it is important for all of us to think about marriage, and how we can support the marriages of our friends and family members.

Today I want to speak of marriage as an intentional commitment for life, publicly proclaimed, most often in our culture officiated by clergy and witnessed by friends and family and God. That is, with some understanding that this very human institution has a transcendent spiritual dimension, as well as an accountability to the larger community. Let me repeat that I include all such unions, including Gay and Lesbian unions, in this definition, even though these unions do not yet have the protection of the civil laws.

But I get a little ahead of myself. Because today, with many of our youth here, I want to take a few moments to talk about the qualities one should look for in a partner. I know some of the youth have heard me talk about this before, but I think it bears repeating today, this close to Valentine's Day. Even though it is always a great mystery how people find and commit to one another, today I will be so bold as to name some basics one should look for in a partner.

I brainstormed these qualities with a friend, with the idea of writing a magazine article. To be clever, we thought of words that began with 'S'. I will alternate pronouns to be inclusive but not cumbersome, so it may require a little translating to fit your life.

Some plain talk about partners: The first quality to look for is Single. This may seem obvious, but sometimes it isn't. Make sure he's single, especially if he's 'not available' on week-ends, or many evenings. And if he's planning to 'separate from his wife' or 'about to file divorce papers', stay away. He's not available. If you're tempted because he's so wonderful, and his marriage, in effect, 'ended a long time ago,' take a taxi home as fast as you can. He's married. He will likely stay married. If he doesn't, he will likely drop you and marry someone else when he's free. Even if you are the 'lucky' one to marry him when his divorce becomes final, could you ever feel secure with a man who had two-timed his wife? Probably not. Don't waste your time.

The second: Sane. There are all levels of sanity. If you had to be totally sane to marry, it's quite possible no one would or could. But if you're attracted to her because she needs you to keep from committing suicide, or her depression is so bad she can't relate to you in any authentic way for weeks at a time, becoming her husband won't help her or you. Be a good friend, but steer clear of romance. She's not what you need.

Solvent. I'm not saying rich, I'm saying solvent. If he's just starting out and has student loans and/or a car loan, but has a regular income, that's promising. If he has plans for expenses and can 'cut back' if he needs to, that's hopeful. If he has no apparent source of income, too many credit card bills, and relies on you to 'help out' when he gets in a bind, watch out. It's not going to get better. It will probably get worse.

Sexy. Yes. Part of the wondrous mystery of love is the force which draws us to one another, and that includes sexual attraction. (I'm not talking about certain over-developed parts of the body, I'm talking about all the wonderful ways one person is with another and feels more alive.) Others will tell you to look beyond sexual attraction in picking a partner. I will be quick to agree. Sexual attraction alone isn't enough to forge a lifelong relationship. But don't tell yourself you can do without it in a relationship. Sexual attraction matters. It's part of the gift of life.

Safe. Do you feel safe with him? Does he regard you with a sense of integrity? Does he take what you say seriously? Is he willing to change his behavior if you ask him to? How do you feel when you are around him? Is he reliable, or does his behavior change erratically from date to date? (Or does it change even during a date due to drink or drugs?) Does he do what he says he will do? Can you count on him? If he hits you, or in any way threatens you, leave. Drunk or sober, remorseful or not, make that the end of the relationship. You don't need it.

Silly. You don't need a clown, but you do need someone who can play and have fun with you. When the going gets rough, a good sense of humor can help. It demonstrates perspective and flexibility. It is taking oneself lightly. Do you laugh together? Is there an element of play in your relationship? If you do, and there is, hold onto her. She may be just what you need.

Service. Does he care about others? It has been said that the measure of a society is its treatment of the poor, the imprisoned, the widows and the children. It follows that the measure of a good person is his treatment of those weaker than he is. Does he give of himself in ways that serve others? This may take time from you, but it will be worth it. It will give your relationship a larger context within which to grow. Maybe you can find a project to work on together as your relationship deepens.

Social. Does she have friends? Does she appreciate your friends? Is your relationship part of a larger circle of friends that you have together? Does she welcome opportunities to do things with other couples you both know? Is there a balance between your private time and social time? Do you feel comfortable when you are out with him? Is he gracious when he meets your friends and family? Does he help make guests comfortable when they are entertained by you? You may be tempted to shut out the 'outside' world when you are first enjoying each other. If you include your friends early in the relationship, you will form a good basis for your social life together.

Sentimental. This may not be high on your list, but it can be very important. A sentimental partner will remember anniversaries and birthdays. She will cherish 'your song.' She will create little rituals that will bring meaning to your lives together. She will notice your preferences, your hopes, your idiosyncrasies, and let you know that she notices. She will keep tokens from dates you have together. And then, when you are old, she will tell loving stories to your grandchildren.

And last, Spiritual. Does he see that something important is between you: something that is not seen, but you know is there and must be tended and nurtured? Does he see your love as a way of knowing a larger love? You will know this more in his regard for life and love than any one particular belief he holds. If he has a church and a faith, does it enlarge his life, or does it make him more narrow and closed? How would you name the spirit with which he approaches his life? Is it a life spirit you respect and honor? If his life includes a regard for life and its larger purposes, it is likely your love will flourish.

I'm sure there are other qualities that partners have that are important to sustaining a marriage. I'm sure there are even more qualities that begin with the letter 'S.' And, I would be willing to bet that at least some of you will spend the remainder of this sermon time thinking up your list. I will enjoy any and all suggestions.

In the scripture I read earlier, I Corinthians 13—read at many weddings and services of union I conduct—is the seed of the remainder of this sermon. It contains a list as well: "Love is patient and kind, love is not jealous or boastful, it is not arrogant or rude. Love does not insist on its own way. It is not irritable or resentful. It does not rejoice at wrong, but rejoices in the right. Love bears all things, believes all things, hopes all things, endures all things." I am always tempted in the middle of weddings to stop to qualify this passage. For Love may be patient and kind, but we often aren't. Love may not be jealous or boastful, but we often are. Love may not insist on its own way, but we often do. Love may not rejoice at wrong, but in our heart of hearts, we may—especially if we are feeling a little beat down by the trials of life. Love may be hopeful and faithful, but we can lose hope, and even fail in our very commitment to love.

This whole chapter, which many read as a description of Love, is actually a description of our finitude. "Now we see in a mirror, dimly," Paul says. "Now I know only in part." And there's the difficulty. Probably there are few places where the paradox of life is more sharply experienced than in marriage. Where our highest hopes for life and our keenest experiences of its difficulties meet.

Thomas Moore says, "because marriage touches upon issues charged with emotion and connected to absolute meaning, it is filled with paradoxical feelings, far-flung fantasies, profound despair, blissful epiphanies, and bitter struggle—all signs of the active presence of soul."[2] This may not be what we expect. The good marriage, we believe, is an intuitive, companionable, loving friendship, with history and good sense thrown in. To imagine the active presence of soul in the full range of joy and despair can be a new idea.

Last week I talked about naming the whirlwind as the essential spiritual practice of Job. Today I will say that naming the whirlwind is also the essential practice of marriage. It is moving within the paradoxes of life and responding authentically within those paradoxes. For, once you have chosen and been chosen—whether it seems by one other, your beloved, or by the great power of Love itself—you enter into one of the most profound paradoxes life offers: living intimately, daily, in the most human reality possible, and embodying Love, the most transcendent quality life gives.

It can make you dizzy. For not only do we see through a glass dimly, but we must look at the same glass early in the morning before public faces are achieved, before social graces are renewed, before spirit and soul are reclaimed. Not only do we see through a glass dimly, but the reflection in the glass is not always what we want.

So how, then, is a good marriage sustained? I will finish with one more list, a shorter one:

First, the paradox of marriage requires that we live embodied love. That we practice the spiritual discipline of love in ways the beloved can receive. They may not be your ways. This is the essential spiritual discipline of attention. It is paying attention to the ways your partner can receive love—not an easy practice. It is the practice of embodied love—making love tangible.

Second, the paradox of marriage requires imagination. I was once leading a workshop on nurturing the spirit while camping—at a conference of Camp Directors in the hills behind Santa Fe. I met a couple there who, after retirement, created a camp for children. All the cabins were tree-houses—they were on raised platforms about 30 feet off the ground. After the conference, we drove to their camp and had coffee at the directors' small home.

The husband, an engineer, had met his wife in Sweden. I asked them how they had met. He told me he had been given a key by a wise older friend when he was a young man, which he had worn around his neck on a chain for many years. He was careful always to wear it, though he wasn't sure why he did so. One day, skiing in some high mountains, he accidentally ran into a woman. They tumbled and tumbled in the snow all the way to the bottom of the hill. When their free fall stopped and they were able to see one another, he could see that she had a tiny lock on a chain around her neck. One that he was sure matched his key. And so they were married.

I must admit I was a little speechless when he stopped the story—caught between the factual nature of my question, and the fantasy of his answer—or at least what I thought was the fantasy of his answer. I wanted to say, "But how did you *really* meet?" But I wisely stifled my request. He had told me. And I realized that whether it was on a snow bank, or on a street corner, or in an engineering office somewhere, it didn't matter. I had the essential quality of their meeting, and understood what he was saying. There they were in their cramped house, building tree houses for children, on an adventure they might never have imagined at the beginning of their marriage. An adventure they might never have attempted, had they not kept imagination alive between them, living a larger story, parts in a drama much greater than their lives.

Living the paradox of marriage requires the intentional spiritual practice of embodied love. Making love tangible. It requires imagination. Not just being clever or creative, but knowing oneself and one's partner as part of the poetic, story-laden imaginative world.

Finally, living paradoxically within marriage is to acknowledge that in our relationships we create space for the sacred. We create places for the sacred to live and move among us. For the most profound intimacy of all is the one in which the sacred dwells. There the spirit of gratitude and awe can arise. It is there that love can abide.

The last three decades have been hard on marriages. The sacred dimension has been made concrete by religion, dictating how one should be, putting limits on the range of allowable feelings and responses within marriage (that is, if people thought there was a sacred dimension at all). Today, the roles which dominated the imagination in fairy tales now don't seem as appropriate. We don't have captivating replacements in our imaginations for Snow White and Prince Charming. The imaginative dimension of marriage has suffered. Less and less have people seen marriage within the context of the larger community, with accountabilities and responsibilities beyond the walls of their homes. And it must be said that the larger society has felt less and less responsible for helping and supporting those in their marriages. Role expectations have changed dramatically, pulling the rug out from under most of what people saw, modeled, and lived. And for Gay and Lesbian people there have been few models of open, supported commitment, cherished and blessed by a religious community, marked by a public ceremony, and honored as they are lived.

The amazing thing is that couples *have* persevered, that love does remain—that this paradoxical, difficult, wondrous institution continues: a gift, a blessing, a place for the deep work of the soul. Not the only place, to be sure, but what a context for our humanity and our spirit to live in!

Valentine's Day, a church holiday in honor of Saint Valentine, is Wednesday. It has become a day for the imagination, a day for romance. A day to make a place for love. I wish for you that it will be a day of blessings. That you will practice love wherever you can that day in imaginative, creative ways. And that married or not, in a relationship or not, love will come back to you ten-fold. Happy Valentine's Day.

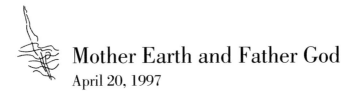

Mother Earth and Father God
April 20, 1997

I would like to revisit this sermon in another ten years to see how we imagine Mother Earth and Father God then. Certainly since this was preached, Rita and Katrina have taught us about fierce mother. Our notion of Fatherhood has changed as well. These deep metaphors are large enough to carry meaning over centuries, and are worthy of our reexamination at regular intervals. LH

Psalm 114, Stephen Mitchell Translation (excerpt)

When Israel went forth from Egypt,
    when a people of slaves was set free,
God was their only guardian,
    the Unnamable was their guide.
The Red Sea saw it and ran back;
    the mighty waters took flight.
Like rams the mountains leaped up;
    the small hills frolicked like lambs.
What made you run back, sea?
    Why did you take flight, waters?
What made you leap, mountains,
    and made the hills frolic like lambs?
The whole earth trembles and dances
    when the God of freedom appears,
who made the rock a clear pool
    and the boulder a bubbling spring.[1]

Earth Teach Me
From the Ute Indians

Earth teach me stillness
    as the grasses are stilled with light.
Earth teach me suffering
    as old stones suffer with memory.
Earth teach me caring
    as parents who secure their young.
Earth teach me courage
    as the tree which stands all alone.
Earth teach me limitation
    as the ant which crawls on the ground.

Earth teach me freedom
   as the eagle which soars in the sky
Earth teach me resignation
   as the leaves which die in the fall.
Earth teach me regeneration
   as the seed which rises in the spring.
Earth teach me to forget myself
   as melted snow forgets its life.
Earth teach me to remember
   kindness as dry fields weep with rain.[2]

I sat at a wedding dinner recently, talking about religion. The man to my right was a Texan who said he was conservative in his religious views. But as he spoke about the need for diversity in our churches, I realized he would not be stereotyped. He was curious, interested in everyone's views; one couldn't presume what he would say. To my left was a Unitarian Universalist from the Northeast, a woman of faith and doubt, articulate, committed to a path of reverence, wonder, and, as she said it, "humility about what she did and did not know." To her left was a man from Iran who had become a Baha'i in the face of what he said was the confusion he felt when he saw Christians, Jews, and Muslims in the city of his birth all say they were the one way, and exclude the others. Baha'i's believe that all prophets are sent by God progressively to bring us to understand that we are one human people in one world, worshipping one God.

Needless to say, it was an interesting conversation. We talked about tolerance, religious practice, the afterlife (was there one and if so, what was it?), the purpose of such teachers as Jesus and Moses, Abraham, and Baha'u'llah—the 19th century divine and teacher of Baha'i. We each were taken to the edge of our beliefs—a not-always-comfortable place to be at a wedding dinner. But we were all connected in an important way by our interest in and commitment to our own faiths.

It was an important conversation to have, as I have thought about this sermon. For the point I wish to make is not a new one, but I needed that reminder to recall its significance. We Unitarian Universalists talk about religious tolerance, tolerance of differences, and understanding of others' views—sometimes rather glibly. But because of our particular faith, which is non-creedal and strives to be non-dogmatic, we walk a very fine line between the dangers, on the one hand, of believing nothing and, on the other hand—and just as potentially vacuous—of believing everything.

We find ourselves often suspended uncomfortably between petty arguments about language and form, and broad sweeping statements about tolerance and understanding. That is why we can be decidedly inarticulate when someone at a dinner party or reception asks, "What do you believe about the afterlife?" "Well, of course, we have no doctrinal statement about the afterlife," we say, "people in Unitarian Universalist churches have many beliefs about that," we go on, as their eyes begin to glaze over.

Of course we have beliefs. Facing our parents' deaths, facing our own, we come to conclusions. Sometimes they change, but as humans, our understanding of death colors our lives, and so it is impossible to live without considering the purpose of our lives and the significance of our individual deaths. Of course we have beliefs! But in the larger scheme of things, we know those beliefs not to be absolute, to be relative to experience, knowledge, and new understandings. And so, at dinner parties and social gatherings, we are careful always to put those understandings in a larger context. We worry about absolutism, about idolatry which says my way is the right way. And so we always start with disclaimers, the ones that cause our dinner partners to look at us askance.

But if you put a bunch of Unitarian Universalist's in a room by ourselves we will not be so vague. The disclaimers will go away. We will speak the truth as we know it, often laced with significant skepticism. We practice, most of the time, a large measure of civility when we talk with each other. It's actually a religious practice for us—civil discourse—speaking our opinion about the subject, but not attacking the person with whom we disagree. Civil discourse is a religious practice, but get us together without people of other faiths, and we're pretty forthright about what we believe, about what we think is or isn't right belief.

And right now—I think I could say this is true—most of us are far more interested in Mother Earth than we are in Father God. We grew up, many of us, with Father God. While for some of us he may have been a Benevolent Father, still he was demanding and patriarchal, to say the least. He was sometimes shaming and, depending on the church of our childhoods, more interested in sin than grace. His justice was often unfair and his ethics sometimes questionable, as he wiped out whole groups of people on behalf of other, chosen groups. He taught us to have dominion over the earth, and at the same time to be subservient to him.

On the other hand, Mother Earth could nurture us at every level, body and spirit: created *with* us rather than over or *against* us. She taught us—especially since we have seen the earth as a bright blue ball from space—that we are all on one earth, living with all her creatures in a delicate balance of mutual coexistence. Mother Earth has much more to teach us, many UU's say, than Father God.

And then this year, in this time thick with religious celebrations all over the world—Buddha's birthday is this month, Muslims are celebrating the Feast of Sacrifice, Eastern Orthodox Christianity is beginning Holy Week today—Passover and Earth Day coincide. This Tuesday, Father God and Mother

Earth meet. Not wanting to mix our religious metaphors, we will have our Seder Dinner this evening, and celebrate Earth Day next Sunday night. Both events will be grand occasions, and important. But on Tuesday, the celebration of Earth Day and the beginning of Passover officially coincide.

We could choose to celebrate one, and ignore the other, whichever suits our taste. But I think it is time we take them as they are. It is time, perhaps, that we *do* mix our religious metaphors and seek the deep truth in both. It is time we re-examined our need for both Mother Earth and Father God lest we, like so many, veer off into our own version of the one path, to the exclusion of all others.

Passover, you will remember, is a celebration of freedom. It has grown out of the story found in the book of Exodus. It is the story of the release of the Israelites from slavery in Egypt. Passover is a ritual re-living of that story. It is understood not only as a remembering of a former time, but as part of a continual process, involving not only the people who celebrate it today, but all those past and future who have and will take part. It is an intergenerational event in the fullest possible sense of the word.

But today—and this is the part where we, who are so grounded in the historical, anthropological, political view of the world have difficulty—the reenactment of the ancient story is not done to remember history. "It is detached", as one Jewish scholar has said, "from its mooring in time."[3]

"Would that it were so," you might say. If it were, we might have less strife in the Middle East today. We might have less oppression, less scarring of the earth. Would that it were truly detached from its mooring in time and from the accounts of history that carry long hurts and generate retaliations over centuries. "If only that could be so." For the metaphors, the stories—at least these deep stories that carry so much power—so easily become imbedded in the politics of the present moment, in the history of vengeance, in the anthropology of territory. How can such a story live with such a weight to carry? How can a Father God bear up under the historical weight of retribution?

It's quite possible that the Father God we knew—and some of us loved and feared in our absolute understanding of him—cannot survive. Just as our understanding of Mother Earth as the benevolent, nurturing, loving, caring and fertile giver of life, is not all there is, either. For just as we cannot imagine a Father who would kill the firstborn of a nation to free others, so, perhaps, we cannot imagine a Mother who would sweep across the plains with floodwaters as she is doing today in the upper Midwest, killing everything in her path.

Our task as a religious people is *not* adoration. That is not what is required. Our task is to see clearly, to understand fully, and to remember always that we see through the glass only dimly, and we only understand in part. Just at the point when we think we've 'got it'—when one understanding fades in favor of another—at that point we must remember, even more intently, that these are all half-gods, partial understandings, small portions of reality.

For the Seder, the story of Passover—a central story for us because it is about freedom—reminds us that all our prior understandings and assumptions are dim shadows of the bright truth. The place at the Seder table is set for Elijah, for the mystery, to arrive. The story itself has given rise to new versions of the Seder. The freedom inherent in the story now allows others to participate. The teaching story becoming the bearer of new truth, as more and more places are prepared at the table.

And, Mother? Mother is becoming more judgmental. She is still as extravagant as always, showering us with her blessings. But her judgments on our wasteful habits, on our inability to share, on our greed, are increasing.

It is time, not only to mix our metaphors a little, to spend time on Tuesday opening ourselves to the Exodus story as a story of liberation for all, and on Earth Day as a story of judgment, as it is time to let go—if only briefly—of our historical, anthropological, political minds, and to sink into the deep truth beyond the words and events portrayed.

Last February I saw a tree such as I had never seen before. I was at a retreat center in California, up in the hills overlooking the ocean. I was leading the retreat and planning a meditation walk when I came upon the tree. It was a Eucalyptus tree at least five feet across—the largest I have ever seen. I was stunned. I sat down on the ground. I went back as often as I could. So did others from the retreat, when they had a chance. It had an overwhelming power. Its roots went deep into the earth, I knew, far beyond my precarious existence on the surface of things. I imagined how many earthquakes, winds, and, perhaps, fires it had sustained over the years. I could see how it swayed with the breezes, its flexibility helping it survive.

It taught me something about my relationship with life that I could not articulate. It was its own metaphor. It was itself and it strengthened me as I stood next to it. Mother Earth, in all her power and glory, was a tree in that moment, and I was a moment in time, existing only to gaze upon it and be glad. But even in that moment, I knew that if I became a worshipper of only a tree, however incredible, I would be diminished. The tolerance of our faith does not come from politeness, or an extreme need to get along, or even from our desire to be inclusive, important as that is. The tolerance of our faith comes from a fierce and deeply held understanding that any belief, however compelling or overwhelming, is, in and of itself, not enough—that every story, every experience is partial, and religion's tendency to claim the partial as the whole is its besetting sin.

As religious people, we grapple with the difficulties of Father God and Mother Earth at the same time, because we must. Because we fear what idolatry of one or the other will do to us. Because we fear what absolute belief in one way (whatever it may be) will create in us.

We have an open, creedless, non-dogmatic faith because it is a human tendency to grasp truth and hold onto it as if it is the only truth, the only experience ever to be given. We have an open, creedless, non-dogmatic faith because a metaphor is so easily literalized, historicized, anthropomorphized, and politicized that the deep mystery the writers and storytellers were trying to convey often gets lost.

We have an open, creedless, non-dogmatic faith because we are in awe of the mystery of life and the small truths and great insights we are given. Because we can sit at a Seder dinner in celebration of human freedom and be nourished. We can have an open faith because there is much, much more to know about God as Father, and Earth as Mother. There is much, much more to learn about living in right relationship with it all.

If there is a God that is in any way like a Father/Mother God, then he/she/it/they smiled on us at that wedding dinner—smiled at our struggle to understand, to know, to reach across the abyss of our individual perceptions. And somewhere in all the differences—in the different stories and even different beliefs, in the midst of all the words—he/she/they found form, not in Baha'i, or Christianity, or even in our Unitarian Universalism, but in between as we reached out, to seek, to find one another.

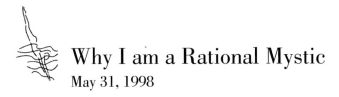

Why I am a Rational Mystic
May 31, 1998

We probably would be better off not defining our theological position, but I can't help myself. As a Rational/Mystic I live out the paradox, keeping one foot in either side of the spectrum. I haven't had anyone try to join me lately to form a group of Rational/Mystics. It's just as well. LH

From *The Dallas Morning News*

With a brain scanner, a University of Pennsylvania scientist eavesdrops on the mind of a meditating Buddhist monk, sifting through the activity of neurons for evidence of spiritual grace.

Using skin sensors, a University of California, San Diego, researcher measures the power of holy words by testing how synapses respond to religious texts.

A neuropsychiatrist at New York University assesses the effects of prayer. Another scientist measures brain function among those who report feelings of a union with God and the cosmos.

Marshaling high-speed medical imaging devices, radioactive tracers and new theories of mental activity, these researchers are probing the neurobiology of religious experience in search of a scientific perspective on the divine . . . .

A number of theologians said they welcomed any scientific insight into spiritual practice. But they also cautioned against any effort to reduce spiritual experience to biochemistry and neurons. Instead, several theologians said, the research is a tangible expression of the mind's own remarkable struggle to know itself.

Mr. Newberg and his colleagues chose to investigate the neurobiology of meditation precisely because it is a spiritual state easily duplicated in the laboratory. The study was funded by the Templeton Foundation, which is interested in fostering ties between science and religion.

So far, they have scanned the brains of nine Buddhist monks during prolonged meditation, and they plan to carry out a similar study of Catholic Franciscan nuns at prayer for comparison.

To photograph the neural activity during meditation, the researchers injected each monk with a faintly radioactive tracer chemical that quickly infuses into brain cells, where it illuminates neural activity for the SPECT camera.

The images reveal distinctive changes in brain activity as the mind settles into a meditative state, Mr. Newberg said. In particular, activity diminished in those parts of the brain involved in generating a sense of three-dimensional orientation in space. The loss of one's sense of place, in turn, could account for a spiritual feeling of release into a place beyond space and time.

This suggests that an essential element of the religious experience of transcendence may be hard-wired in the brain . . . .

From the *Book of Job*

Then the Lord answered Job out of the whirlwind:
Who is this that darkens counsel by words without knowledge?
Gird up your loins like a man, I will question you, and you shall declare to me.
"Where were you when I laid the foundation of the earth?
Tell me, if you have understanding,
Who determined its measurements
    —surely you know!
Or who stretched the line upon it?
On what were its bases sunk,
or who laid its cornerstone,
when the morning stars sang together,
and all the sons of God shouted for joy?
Or who shut in the sea with doors,
when it burst forth from the womb;
when I made clouds its garment,
and thick darkness its swaddling band,
and prescribed bounds for it,
and set bars and doors,
and said, "Thus far shall you come,
and no farther,
and here shall your proud waves be stayed?"
Have you commanded the morning since your days began,
and caused the dawn to know its place,
that it might take hold of the skirts of the earth,
and the wicked be shaken out of it?

Have you entered into the springs of the sea,
or walked in the recesses of the deep?
Have the gates of death been revealed to you,
or have you seen the gates of deep darkness?

Have you comprehended the expanse of the earth?
Declare, if you know all this.
Where is the way to the dwelling of light,
and where is the place of darkness . . . .
Can you bind the chains of the Pleiades,
    Or loose the cords of Orion?
Can you lead forth the Mazzaroth in their season,
    Or can you guide the Bear with its children?
. . .
Can you lift up your voice to the clouds,
    that a flood of waters may cover you?
Can you send forth lightenings, that they may go and say to you,
'Here we are'?
Who has put wisdom in the clouds,
    Or given understanding to the mists?

The phrase "rational mystic" came originally from the very practical need to have something to put into those blanks that always show up on theological school forms, on forms for the denomination, and often as the first question of a search committee when a minister is being considered for a position. At first, I was rather flippant. I thought the juxtaposed and somewhat paradoxical phrase rather clever, if I did say so myself.

I didn't want to get caught in what had been a constant and not always polite categorizing of students in our theological schools—categorized simply by whether they were humanists or theists (often, I've been told, the first question asked a new student)—placing him or her (it was almost always him in those days) on one side or the other of a line firmly drawn, and which would last all of his theological school days. I didn't want to get caught in one of those traps, though I would say that today the categories would be more varied, if not perhaps equally as limiting. So it was, with some effort at being perplexing enough not to be pinned down, that I began to use the phrase "rational/ mystic" to describe my theological position.

After I preached my first sermon on the topic, not too long after I arrived here, I received a letter from a colleague saying that he had read the sermon, and wanted me to know that there was one other colleague of ours who also called himself a rational/ mystic. He was sending my sermon on, he told me, and after that we did have some correspondence. I will admit that I was slightly disappointed that I hadn't thought of it first. The minister who made my theological position a movement of two was older than I, and retired. Perhaps he cherished some similar disappointment, and our correspondence waned.

But then the blow really hit. I had already announced this title this year, when reading up on the sermon I preached two weeks ago, I came across a reference to the works of the Neo-Platonists in the area of rational mysticism. Now mind you, this is around 205 C.E. So much for originality! But, even though it was a blow to discover that I hadn't been the first, and that the rational/mystic idea had come down through almost 2000 years of philosophical and religious tradition, it felt good to drive a stake into history. To mark it. To see the roots of what I perhaps only intuitively had known. Or what I had learned and then forgotten, and thought was my own new idea.

In any case, let me tell you what you may already know, and perhaps like me, have forgotten. Incidentally, I appreciate your indulgence if you have known all along that I was not the first. You are kind. Plato identified the intellect with the Divine. Knowing was to Know (capital K). Those who followed Plato (and these are my Neo-Platonist rational/mystics) took it one step further—believing that we could introspectively confront the immanent God in our souls. As Sydney Ahlstrom says in the introduction to the book, *An American Reformation: A Documentary History of Unitarian Christianity*, "Here Hellenic (Greek) thought comes full circle: for here in the mystical confrontation of God comes empirical knowledge."

A lot happens, of course, between the work of the Neo-Platonists and the reforms of Luther and Calvin. But the thread of rational-mysticism (not invented ten years ago by me, unfortunately, but continued into the 16th century by our religious ancestors who participated in the radical reformation)—the thread continued. Ahlstrom says, " . . . the appearance of the post-Reformation heroes of the Unitarian Reformation must be considered. The inspiration of these liberals came from various quarters . . . mysticism from Platonic influences, the new emphasis on practical, this-world morality; and naturalistic outlook of scientific investigators." [3]

I call myself a rational/mystic because I want to make sure that *you* understand that by mystic I don't mean floating off into the world of the supernatural. I think natural life is astounding enough without needing anything super-natural to divert our attention or lure our loyalty away from the present. By mystic I mean those things experienced which can only be described allegorically or symbolically. Like the experience of oneness the scientists are now measuring neurologically as Buddhists meditate, or Catholics pray. It can perhaps be measured, but it cannot be described, except by metaphor, by poetry, and in relational ways.

I call myself a rational/mystic because I want to make sure that *you* understand that by rational I don't mean linear, positivist (what you see is what you get) kind of literal absolutism. Because that is not what I mean by rational.

It is an irony in our time that religion, in many forms, has become increasingly literal in its self-understanding and pronouncements, while science has become more metaphorical. What are *quarks*, after all, but metaphors for a reality that is experienced and measured by physicists but described by metaphor. Much of what is called *religion* in our time is more of a pseudo-scientism than religion. It is as if somewhere they passed in the night—science and religion—in the ways they describe their understandings, in the ways they describe truth.

Because the question of *how we know*, how we know the truth of our lives, the truth of Life itself, is not off in some dusty corner, left to molder while we tend to the more important issues of life. The question of how we know truth is as important to us as it was to Plato, to the Neo-Platonists, to those of our religious ancestors (Ahlstrom calls them "Unitarian heroes") in the Western rational tradition, who said reasonable proof was necessary, more than demanding acceptance from the faithful.

When you (some of you) were told in your Sunday Schools, in answer to your questions "you only have to believe" or "you have only to have faith," and you, in your heart of hearts, and mind of minds, said to yourself or perhaps even to your teacher "I don't think so," you were living the difference between a tradition of faithful acceptance and a rational tradition of truth (as Emerson would say), "as life experience passed through the fire of thought."[4]

My son had his first experience in graduate school as a teacher's assistant this last quarter, teaching a group of undergraduates at UCLA about linguistics. "How is it going?" I asked him a few weeks ago. "Oh, fine," he said. "They're a bright group and it's interesting, except when I've taught them about something, and a student asks 'Is that *really* true?'" I think when you are teaching a section of undergraduates and they ask that question, the answer is "yes." If you are preaching in a free church of a liberal faith, the answer is "yes and no." For truth, as we know it, is qualified, influenced by other perceptions of truth, never fully known in its entirety, whether you are a rationalist or a mystic. The two historical paths, that of the rational tradition and that of the mystical tradition, seem to be diametrically opposed—one based on critical thought of the highest order, on "checking your sources," as one of my professors once said, being meticulously careful about your sources, your experiments, even your theories, and using all the powers of critical thought to come the closest to truth as you can. And the other practicing a catholicity of spirit, an openness to the experience of Life in ways you might never have imagined.

That is why, today, in this somewhat cumbersome explanation (after all, *"Why I Am a Rational/Mystic"* is a question a person in the rational tradition would ask), I find the use of the words of God in answer to Job's torment alongside the scientific explorations of what happens neurologically when Buddhists and others pray and meditate and have "mystical experiences of oneness with all" . . . I find the juxtapositions of this ancient scripture, this scribe who puzzles out the question of the truth of life in Job (what's it all for, anyway?) alongside these modern explorers of truth with their neurological testing, rather elegant in their pairing.

Then the Lord answered Job out of the whirlwind . . .

> "Where were you when I laid the foundation of the earth?
> Tell me, if you have understanding . . .
> who laid its cornerstone,
> when the morning stars sang together,
> and all the sons of God shouted for joy?"[5]

"Where were you?" Tell me, if you know. And I know that at Stanford's Linear Accelerator a "B factory", a facility that will allow physicists to study the behavior of "B's"—asymmetrical sub-atomic particles—will give us, they hope, the clues to why there is matter. Because these asymmetrical particles are the key, they believe, to why matter prevailed over anti-matter.

"Where were you?" God asks Job. Well, we weren't there, but we may just be able to figure out what happened. We might not have been there, but we will know the truth of it. The rational Western tradition has taught us to know in ways we could never even have imagined a century ago, when this church was being built. And the poetry of the writer of Job, says:

> "Or who shut in the sea with doors,
> when it burst forth from the womb;
> when I made clouds its garment,
> and thick darkness its swaddling band"[6]

And we're impressed to find the depths of the ocean contain more creatures than we have ever imagined.

We cannot let go of the poetry which brings layer upon layer of knowing of the heart and mind of life. The intuitive experience of wholeness and peace which goes beyond our daily lives. The prayer and meditation which they may find changes our neurons, but for sure changes our lives. As we get closer and closer to knowing, perhaps even the origins of the universe, the genetic basis of our humanity—all gifts of the Western Rational tradition—let us not even begin to think we have known the mind and heart of God or Life, or begun to touch the depths of truth in the poetry of Job.

I am a rational mystic because knowing the truth is important to me, not so I can practice faithful acceptance, but so that I can be in relationship with a living truth, a dynamic truth, truth that courses through my body in DNA, and rises up from my heart and mind in poetry. The truth I experience, the truth that calls me forward, the truth that, beyond all I know, sets me free.

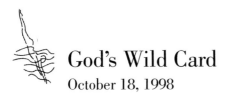

God's Wild Card
October 18, 1998

It is hard for those of us who depend upon the life of the mind for most of our orientation in life, to admit to the parts that are out of control. This sermon calls us to the joy in that 'wildness.' It is remembered as a favorite. LH

The Rowing Endeth
By Anne Sexton

I'm mooring my rowboat
at the dock of the island called God.
This dock is made in the shape of a fish
and there are many boats moored
at many different docks.
"It's okay," I say to myself,
with blisters that broke and healed
and broke and healed—saving
themselves over and over.
And salt sticking to my face and arms like
a glue-skin pocked with grains of tapioca.
I empty myself from my wooden boat
and onto the flesh of The Island.

"On with it!" He says and thus
we squat on the rocks by the sea
and play—can it be true—a
game of poker.
He calls me.
I win because I hold a royal straight flush.
He wins because He holds five aces.

A wild card had been announced
but I had not heard it
being in such a state of awe
when He took out the cards and dealt.
As he plunks down His five aces
and I sit grinning at my royal flush,
He starts to laugh,

the laughter rolling like a hoop out of His mouth
and into mine,
and such laughter that He doubles right over me
laughing a Rejoice Chorus at our two triumphs.
Then I laugh, the fishy dock laughs
the sea laughs. The Island laughs.
The Absurd laughs.

Dearest dealer,

I with my royal straight flush,
love you so for your wild card,
that untamable, eternal, gut-driven ha-ha
and lucky love.[1]

I must admit that until I read the Anne Sexton's poem, I had never thought of God as a poker player. Growing up as a Baptist, I never thought much about poker! I remember as a high school Junior having to have some tutoring in my Algebra class. When we came to the section on probabilities, I did not know the suits in a deck of cards—which was essential knowledge to be able to do the problems.

I had never thought much about poker, to say nothing about *God* as a poker player. For a Baptist, this does not rise unbidden into one's consciousness. Of all the small gods that commanded my loyalty, as well as those I didn't believe in, none of them were poker players. It is easy to think of life as a game, with rules and stakes and strategies. But somehow, sitting on the rocks by the sea, playing a game of poker with God—somehow that had not crossed my mind, ever, as a useful picture of my relationship with ultimate reality, or simply, "How it is with us." Until I read that poem. For isn't it true? There you are with a Royal Straight Flush—ace, king, queen, jack, 10—all of the same suit. So in awe that you're even *in* the game that you don't notice a wild card has been called.

Of course the truth of our lives is that the wild card was called long ago—long before we, or any history that we remember, existed. It's just that we tend to forget about it until it's played. "Life is not illogicality," G.K. Chesterton once said, "Yet it is a trap for logicians. It looks just a little more mathematical and regular than it is; its exactitude is obvious; but its inexactitude is hidden; *its wildness lies in wait.*"[1]

And so we order our days. Much of the time we can be reasonably sure that if we do one thing, another will follow. Our very sanity depends on that being largely true. Much of the skill of living comes in predicting what will come next, in perceiving, even within its nuances and complexities, life's predictability. But while most of our world is orderly (we do live and move and have our beings in fairly predictable ways) not all of it is. For inevitably, in spite of all our efforts to the contrary, we encounter the wildness which "lies in wait."

I know I'm not telling you anything new. I would wager that many of you were initially drawn to Unitarian Universalism because it is in our midst that you were able to acknowledge the wildness, the unpredictability of life. It is here that we face, as best we can, the incongruities, the paradoxes of life openly, honestly. It is here, as best we can, we keep our beliefs, our sense of things, open. Supported by one another and, in an ironic way, by trust and faith, we are prepared to take what comes.

I know I am not telling you anything new, but there is more that needs to be said. For we who are so concerned that we live out the full dimensions of life and truth often acknowledge only part of the truth about the wildness of life. It is true that when this wildness comes to us it often wounds us, leaving us bruised and scarred. It is true that this wildness often gives rise to our fears and turns our fears into realities. But it is also true that the wildness of life is the source of our laughter, our joy—the source of richness of spirit and fullness of life.

We know this—intuitively, at least. It is often why young people, and not a few people old enough to know better, try wildness as a way of life. Wanting to appropriate this element of life as their own, to control it, to manage it, to become it, in an odd kind of idolatry. But the wildness of God, the unexpected which wounds or enriches, cannot be managed, cannot be appropriated by wild living, wild appearance, by taking some small form of wildness as a companion. This wildness of life in my meaning today cannot be appropriated, cannot be put on as a garment or life-style. It has nothing to do with purple hair or body piercings or tattoos, or what society might name as wild behavior. This wildness comes to us—young or old, conventional or not—unbidden and unexpected. This is the wildness of life itself.

Consider, for example, the absurdity of life. Much of life can appear absurd. There are many large things about the reality of our lives that don't make much sense, not the least of which is that we must invest all that we have in living, with the inevitability that we will die. Most of the time, even though to some degree we must acknowledge the absurdity in life, we manage to live and work with a sense of meaning and purpose. But then, once in awhile, absurdity rises up—the wild card that was called so long ago is named—and drains the color, the meaning, the purpose from our days. "Why bother," we might think. "What does it matter?" we might believe.

But on Anne Sexton's fishy dock a wild card is named, and the *absurd* laughs. At the moment of triumph a wild card is named and there is a double triumph. Now, *that* is absurd! Because in the game of poker as I understand it, someone wins and someone loses. *This* is the strange thing. *This* is the paradox: that we who are so familiar with the wildness inherent in all of life, especially in its more tragic forms, frequently are blinded to the possibility of rejoice-choruses of laughter—the "gut-driven ha-ha" which arises out of that very same wildness.

When I stand next to a woman of obvious means as through a window we watch our cars move through a car wash (this did happen to me) and she turns to me, a perfect stranger, and says, "You know, just once, I'd love to go through there in a convertible with the top down," I am startled. The absurd laughs. We talk among ourselves of openness, and we are amazingly open with one another. It is a source of great vitality in our faith. But I wonder sometimes if our openness to the wildness of the shadow side of life has left us vulnerable to closing ourselves off to the wildness that is light, that is joy, the wildness that is laughter. The wildness that is love.

Sometimes I think we are more skilled at coping with the tragic disjunctures and incongruities of our lives than with the startling and amazing double-rejoice-chorus surprises. We, who are skilled at grappling with problems which come our way, unexpected though they may be, sometimes have trouble receiving the surprises of life when, disorienting though they often are, we are *not* called to wrestle, to contend, to cope. When we are only to receive, and be changed. How many of us, at least at some level, when something good, *really* good happens to us, either say or think that we'd better start looking over our shoulders, expecting the other shoe to drop, with nary a thought for a double rejoice chorus?

Some of you may remember Charles Dutton. A wonderful young man, active in the church. I did not realize for a long time that he was HIV positive, or how inevitable it was that he would convert to a full-blown case of AIDS. Not long before he died, he told me that even though it made little sense in the scheme of things, that he believed having AIDS was the best thing that had ever happened to him. That at some point in his recognition of the absurdity, the tragedy of it, he realized that he had discovered what it meant to live, and it brought him great joy.

It defines a skepticism peculiar to our time, and perhaps a skepticism peculiar to our faith—our no-nonsense faith—but it is a skepticism that keeps us from dreaming, from hoping, from imagining that we live in a kingdom where double rejoice choruses could be the norm. We do live in a world that we perceive as largely ordered, which usually functions in reasonable and predictable ways. But we know, as Garrison Keillor of "Prairie Home Companion" radio fame said, "The world we thought was tucked in neatly like a sheet is unfinished and incomplete."

The incompleteness of it, the wildness of it, is what calls us forward to action, to courage, to great faith in the face of chaos and tragedy. But it is in the wildness, too—and we must not forget this—where we find that untamable, eternal gut-driven ha-ha and lucky love. For it is one thing to call a wild card—that was done long ago, before anyone was able even to be in awe of it. It is another, if I have the rules to Poker right, to *name* the wild card. You don't name it, as I understand the game, you don't name it until you play it. Perhaps that is where we need to focus our attention—in the *naming* of the wildness that comes our way.

Anne Sexton moors her little boat with blisters that "broke and healed, and broke and healed, saving themselves over and over". How many of us have the scars to prove we've done that? With the salt from the sweat and work of life sticking to our skin. She squats on the rocks by the sea and plays a game of poker with God. She wins because she has a royal straight flush.

Don't we all, in some unaccountable way, hold those same cards? Hard to believe, but we are here, we are alive, we are living this great gift. She holds a royal straight flush. And he wins because he holds five aces. What a game. What an absurd game!

But if we have eyes to see, we know that is the game we are in. It is the one described by the Psalmists. It is the one we remember when we laugh at an unexpected comment in a car wash by a stranger. It is what we know when we remember that our partners and friends are unfathomable mystery to be discovered and discovered and discovered. When we see that dying is another strange but amazing chapter in living. It is gratitude, it is breath, it is joy.

> "Dearest dealer,
> [*What a name for God!*]
> I with my royal straight flush,
> Love you so for your wild card,
> That untamable, eternal, gut-driven ha-ha
> And lucky love."

So may it be.

How to Help Your Child
Have A Spiritual Life
July 25, 1999

*I believe the message of this sermon more now than I could have
when I preached it. I've been at the church long enough now to see
some of the children grow up, marry, and have children of their own.
It's my experience that if we're straight-talking with them, and help
them build on what they already know about themselves and about
their faith, they will stick with us. One of our college students, home
for a break said to me, "You never talked down to us." I consider that
a high compliment. It does matter what we believe, what we do, and
what we say. It matters a lot. LH*

It Matters What We Believe
By Sophia Lyon Fahs

Some beliefs are like walled gardens. They encourage exclusiveness, and the feeling of being especially privileged. Other beliefs are expansive and lead the way into wider and deeper sympathies.

Some beliefs are like shadows, clouding children's days with fears of unknown calamities. Other beliefs are like sunshine, blessing children with the warmth of happiness.

Some beliefs are divisive, separating the saved from the unsaved, friends from enemies. Other beliefs are bonds in a world community, where sincere differences beautify the pattern.

Some beliefs are like blinders, shutting off the power to choose one's own direction. Other beliefs are like gateways opening wide vistas for exploration.

Some beliefs weaken a person's selfhood. They blight the growth of resourcefulness. Other beliefs nurture self-confidence and enrich the feeling of personal worth.

Some beliefs are rigid, like the body of death, impotent in a changing world. Other beliefs are pliable, like the young sapling, ever growing with the upward thrust of life.[1]

From *The Prophet*
By Kahlil Gibran

> Your children are not your children.
> They are the sons and daughters of life's longing for itself.
> They come through you but not from you,
> and though they are with you yet they belong not to you.
> You may give them your love but not your thoughts,
> for they have their own thoughts.
> You may house their bodies but not their souls,
> for their souls dwell in the house of tomorrow,
> which you cannot visit,
> not even in your dreams.
>
> You may strive to be like them,
> but seek not to make them like you.
> For life goes not backward nor tarries with yesterday.
> You are the bows from which your children as living arrows are sent forth.
> The Archer sees the mark upon the path of the infinite,
> and bends you with might that the arrows may go swift and far.
> Let your bending in the Archer's hand be for gladness.[2]

Last Saturday, in the religion section of the Dallas Morning news, a rather chilling article greeted us. It was titled, "Children of the End Times" and featured a movement within the Pentecostal Church—which has grown exponentially in recent years—to train children as young as toddlers to be "Warriors for God." The article described parents who believe that training their children in prayer and Bible study can armor them with the Holy Spirit. They believe that Satan is killing this generation of children, through abortion and through the general destruction of society by violence, moral failings and anarchy in the schools. They believe their children may be the last generation on the earth before the return of Christ.

The article goes on to describe their presentations to children, especially at North Church in Carrollton, where the room for 100 elementary age school kids has a sound system and an area for costume changes and puppet storage. In another room, the "Bible Fact" man, a member of the congregation painted green, got the pre-school children's attention by having them pretend they were growing grass. "How do you grow?" he asked them. "By reading the Bible!" they replied. The fifth and sixth graders' "High Voltage" class was learning about the end times and their literal belief in the rapture, when Jesus will swoop down and lift them into the clouds. "What if your mom, dad, sister and brother were left behind?" the teacher asks.

Traditional Pentecostalism, a highly emotional religion, coupled with societal fears and focused on Y2K—the threatened disintegration of the structures of our society when our computers go down as the new millennium begins—has given rise, (once again, I would add) to an intense, highly emotional, fear-based religion for children. It has not been so long since Jonathan Edwards preached, in the mid-1700s, his famous sermon "Sinners in the Hands of an Angry God" in which he described a man hanging over a dark abyss by a thread. It is said that one man, so overwhelmed by the sermon, left the church and committed suicide.

I would be among the first to say that fear has its place. It alerts us to potentially dangerous situations. It makes us alert in moments when we need to be alert. But fear coupled with religion, especially when it is given to children as a package, can be a powerful force. I will admit that when I read this article, I felt a chill of fear for those children. I know, at least in part, what it is like to take seriously a religion that pits itself against a society that is to be feared, on behalf of a God who is fearsome as well.

For, while I didn't grow up in the emotionality of Pentecostalism, I did grow up in a Fundamentalist church where I learned to be good to secure my salvation—which, though promised, was never quite assured in my own mind.

In this religion, I was afraid for my father's salvation, who I was not sure was saved. I was afraid to reach out into the world as I grew because the world was a threat to be avoided. I could identify, unfortunately, with the little five year old praying fervently in her "Extreme for Jesus" class at The North Church, in the lead photo of the article in the paper.

This article has made it difficult for me to speak about the subject I had planned today, "How to Help Your Child Have a Spiritual Life," because so much of what we do seems to be in response to this kind of fear-instilling, perfection-seeking, over-responsible doctrine: a doctrine that was preached to some of us as children and is taught in churches not far from here today.

For in reaction to such emotionalism, it can be easy to make our religion bland; in reaction to such literalism, it can be easy to skip over traditional religious teachings and stories; in reaction to such fervent perfectionism, it can be easy to let children go their own way, not challenged or inspired by us. In reaction to religion as control, it can be easy to assume no responsibility for our children's understanding of what is good and right to do in the world. In reaction to an over-zealous piety, it can be easy to pretend that our children are not religious beings, needing our guidance as they ask the large questions of meaning and purpose—who God is, and where to find solace in times of grief and suffering.

As frightening as the movement to turn toddlers into "Warriors for God" and "Children of the End Times" is, we can be comforted by the reality that this is not the first time such movements have risen up among us in this country. (If you're interested, read up on the First Great Awakening, and then the Second Awakening; and note that our faith had an answer then, and has an answer today.)

Quite simply, our Universalist ancestors, who flourished in response to the likes of Jonathan Edwards, said, "God is love." This was no pabulum to comfort the frightened sinner. This was a deeply held response to a theology of fear. "God is love," they simply said. It doesn't mean that everything is great. It means that God is not suspending you by a thread over a dark abyss unless you repent. It means you are sheltered in the hands of a loving God, no matter what.

It was a doctrine of liberation, of freedom, of universal redemption. It was a doctrine of love. It is not an accident that we begin our affirmation each week with the words, "Love is the doctrine of our church." It *is*. It is not something we conjure up. It is a gift. God loves us.

I would be so bold as to say that our children should learn, "Jesus loves me/This I know/For the Bible tells me so. Little ones to him belong/They are weak but he is strong. Yes Jesus loves me. Yes Jesus loves me. Yes Jesus loves me. The Bible tells me so." For our youngest, this simple message of trust is wonderfully Universalist and appropriate.

It was Hosea Ballou's careful reading of the Bible (out behind the barn and away from his stern father's eye) that convinced him that nowhere did it say that God would send people to hell. It was his reading of the Bible that convinced him that God was love, and sent him abroad in the land preaching the Universalist, and, for that time, radical doctrine.

"Jesus loves me" to my mind, is a Universalist song that our children should learn to sing. And yet many of us have difficulty with the idea. For one thing, not all of us are Christians. We worry that, in our pluralistic world, using the language of a traditional Christian faith might limit our children's understanding. And then there is the concern that our children would mistakenly think we believe in the same Jesus that the North Church is teaching. Would the language blind them to the difference between a fear-based and a love-based religion?

I believe it is our fears about these questions that have limited our ability to help our children have a spiritual life.

We teach Bible stories at this church. We teach stories of other religions. We teach stories of our own heritage, and stories are the way the wisdom of the fathers and mothers are passed to the next generations. But if we do not teach "Jesus loves me" or its equivalent—if we do not teach how to be in relationship with life, with God, with Jesus, with our deepest, wisest self—we have taught only the head and not nurtured the heart of our children.

The antidote to a regular dose of hellfire and brimstone preaching for me as a child was my deeply held belief that Jesus loved me. Little did I know that I was learning good Universalist doctrine, and that as an adult I would speak it each Sunday as part of the affirmation of my church.

Let me suggest another Christian song. Hardy Sanders told me this story, and I'm sure won't mind me telling it. He says that as a little boy growing up in the Methodist Church in Crowell Texas, they sang, "Jesus loves the little children/all the children of the world/red and yellow black and white, they are precious in his sight. Jesus loves the little children of the world." Hardy said he guessed the problem was *he believed it*, and has lived it all his life in his commitment to desegregation in this city and to helping all children as best he could.

What I am saying is that to help our children have a spiritual life—and I'm speaking of the children of this church, whether they are yours individually or not—we have to get over our fear of religious language.

Remember when someone (probably our parents) warned, "If you cross your eyes, they'll get stuck that way!" We learned that wasn't true. We need to learn now that if our children think there is a real Jesus, and that he really loves them as a kind of invisible friend who protects them from monsters under the bed, that's okay. They won't be destined to be literalists all their lives. Not in this church. Not in our homes.

James Fowler, who has studied how faith is developed in children and adults, has made the liberating and helpful observation that people grow in stages quite naturally in relation to their religious surroundings. If their church, for example, is a fundamentalist, literal one, they probably will continue that belief all their lives. If they are challenged by others along the way in their faith communities, they will be more likely to change their beliefs and understandings as they age.

This is to say that it is very important that we give our littlest children stories and songs which assure them in concrete ways that God loves them, that having trusting open hearts is good, that caring for others is important. As they grow we need to be very aware of when the concrete understandings can be opened up—when paradox, irony, and metaphor can begin to be an important element of faith.

Little children should be taught to pray. And we need to be prepared when they pray for what they want and hope they will magically get, and not worry about it. They are learning to express their yearnings. There will be plenty of time for them to broaden their understanding of what their deepest yearnings are—the ones that carry them forward in meaning and purpose.

Our children should be taught poems and scripture so that they will have wisdom words within their hearts throughout their lives. It is important that they be able to move comfortably among the world's great religions, but it is even more important that they know themselves as religious people—as having "thou" relationships with people they know, with nature, and with the holy in life. If we teach religion only as an interesting topic for study, we will run the danger of raising skeptics, of raising the next generation to embody our ambivalence and lack of clarity about our religious natures.

Someone said to me recently, "We keep our children hidden away in the Religious Education building." I've been thinking about that a lot lately. It is true that we want to find better ways for all of us to worship together, to play together, to get to know one another in our families.

But I have decided that the children are not hidden in the RE building. It is we who are hiding, we who are reluctant to share our lives with them, to share our faith with them. To pray with them and speak in concrete terms about God and love and service. To help our older children build on a base of faith and face the polarities in their lives which seem always in tension—the paradoxes in life which are unresolvable. To help all of them learn the trust in life that is the basis of healthy relationships. It is we who have been hiding, we who leave it up to other parents to teach the children, to the paid caregivers to take care of the babies.

We (many of us) have been hiding because we haven't known what to say, coming from no church, or wanting not to do it the way we were raised, but not knowing what to do or say. We have been hiding, not because we don't care about our children, but because we care so much we don't want to mess it up.

How do you help your child have a spiritual life? The first step is to acknowledge that you have one yourself. That Love is God here. Practicing expressing our love in concrete ways is a way to love God back. Gratitude is our response to the gifts we receive. Praying our thanks together is a concrete way to express our gratitude. Serving others together as a family is a way to express our care. Learning wisdom words, and talking about scripture and poems together is a way of promoting wise living in our children.

As Clarke Wells, Unitarian Universalist minister, once said of the fervent fundamentalists, "Don't worry. We will build churches in their wake." Such fear does not sustain people. Such fervent emotionalism does not nourish an already over-stimulated generation of children.

Let us not allow our fear to make us vague, reluctant, skeptical and unhelpful. Let us not hide from our children when it comes to their spiritual lives. They need us.

The Good News: You're Not Crazy
August 6, 2000

I didn't realize, until I delivered this sermon, that there are two kinds of people who think they might be crazy: (1) the ones who have never known Unitarian Universalism existed and they are the only people who think the way they do; and (2) the ones who never expected themselves to be in church and whose friends think they're crazy because they are. This sermon was a hit with both groups. LH

Why I make Sam go to Church (excerpt)
By Anne Lamott

Sam is the only kid he knows who goes to church—who is made
to go to church two or three times a month. He rarely wants to. This
is not exactly true: the truth is he *never* wants to go. What young boy
would rather be in church on the weekends than hanging out with a
friend? It does not help him to be reminded that once he's there he
enjoys himself, that he gets to spend the time drawing in the little
room outside the sanctuary, that he only actually has to sit still and
listen during the short children's sermon. It does not help that I always
pack some snacks, some legos, his art supplies, and bring along any
friend of his whom we can lure into our churchy web. It does not
help that he genuinely cares for the people there. All that matters to
him is that he alone among his colleagues is forced to spend Sunday
morning in church.

You might think, noting the bitterness, the resignation, that he
was being made to sit through a six-hour Latin mass. Or you might
wonder why I make this strapping, exuberant boy come with me most
weeks, and if you were to ask, this is what I would say.

I make him because I can. I outweigh him by nearly seventy-five
pounds.

But that is only part of it. The main reason is that I want to give
him what I found in the world, which is to say a path and a little light
to see by. Most of the people I know who have what I want—which
is to say, purpose, heart, balance, gratitude, joy—are people with a
deep sense of spirituality. They are people in community, who pray,
or practice their faith; they are Buddhists, Jews, Christians—people
banding together to work on themselves and for human rights. They
follow a brighter light than the glimmer of their own candle; they are
part of something beautiful. I saw something once from the Jewish
Theological Seminary that said, "A human life is like a single letter

of the alphabet. It can be meaningless. Or it can be a part of a great meaning . . .

When I was at the end of my rope, the people at (my church) tied a knot in it for me and helped me hold on. The church became my home in the old meaning of *home*—that it's where, when you show up, they have to let you in. They let me in. They even said, "You come back now."[1]

From *Gitanjali, A Collection of Indian Songs*
By Rabindranath Tagore

I thought that my voyage had come to its end at the last limit of my power—that the path before me was closed, that provisions were exhausted and the time come to take shelter in a silent obscurity.

But I find that thy will knows no end in me. And when old words die out on the tongue, new melodies break forth from the heart; and where the old tracks are lost, new country is revealed with its wonders.[2]

The good news: you're not crazy. Sometimes I think the opposite is true. We're *all* crazy; some of us just hide it better than others. But, this sermon will not attempt to define who is, and who isn't crazy. I leave that to others.

I'm not being entirely facetious, however, when I attempt to reassure you. Because many people come to this place, thinking that they are. Crazy. Especially when it comes to religion. The black sheep of their families, they have come to a place which no one could have predicted back in Sunday School, or Catechism classes, or at confirmation, or your Bar or Bat Mitzvah. And that was the place when you decided that what it seemed everyone else believed, wasn't true.

James Fowler—who has spent most of his career figuring out what he calls "Stages of Faith"—says it was a moment in mass in his Catholic church, with his girlfriend. She was a year older, and she had come home after her first year of college. In the middle of mass, she turned to him and said, "This is an ancient totemic ritual, you know." That was the moment everything changed.

For some of you it was one Sunday when, in the middle of the Apostle's Creed, you couldn't say the words. You realized, in the midst of all those statements of belief, that you didn't believe.

For me it was an off-hand remark by my college boyfriend. He said of our conservative church: "I don't think they want us to read books." I knew he meant the books *we* were reading. A "click" went off in my head. It was true. And at that point, all the old favorite comforting hymns—"There is a fountain filled with blood, drawn from Emanuel's veins"—became strange, and actually rather macabre. I felt odd, suddenly cast out. Not by my church but by an internal knowing that would not let me stay. I did not know it at the time, but I had become a heretic, a nonconformist, a dissenter. Actually part of a noble, historical tradition. I did not know it at the time, but I was not crazy.

I remember my mother asking me what I believed about Jesus. When I told her I wasn't sure, she wept. She knew, perhaps better than I, that "not being sure" would puncture my cohesive, understandable, dependable world. She knew, perhaps better than I, the pain my lack of surety would bring. Looking back, I can say it was an exquisite kind of pain. It carried with it a sense of adventure, a way of being alive, an autonomy that was both wearing and exhilarating.

These were the heady days when the possibilities for women were suddenly bound only by the limits of our courage. You could "go it alone." It wasn't easy, but it could be done. Superstition was what limited progress. And selfishness. These were the days of the Peace Corps, and our belief that the world could be made fair and all her people one, if we were committed enough. And we believed that the more we could know, the less there would be need for God, because there would be less mystery.

I don't want to imply that this is all in the past-tense, because I still believe we can make the world a better place, and that knowledge will help, not hinder us. I still remain astounded that there is a religious tradition, where, even with my doubts about Jesus, and my love of knowledge, and my determination not to be superstitious, and my at-the-time-somewhat naïve sense that the world could be made much, much better for everyone—there was a place where I was not crazy. There was a place where I could be human, and know I was loved. Just loved. No guilt, no striving. Just loved. That's what our Universalist ancestors gave us. God's love. Unencumbered.

You're *not* crazy if that's what brought you here. If the freedom to forge one's relationship with the ultimacies of life—birth, death, meaning, purpose—is given you here. If the permission to search deeply and widely for the ways you will become more yourself, the gift that was simple possibility at your conception. If being blessed as who you are, not who you must be. If the freedoms forged by our religious ancestors at great sacrifice to themselves are what brought you here. If simply the sense that you are not crazy brought you here to be among so many of us who once thought we were the only ones who thought this way. Then welcome. You're in the right place.

That was my plan for my sermon today. A welcome to the free church, the free tradition. A noble, heretical religious tradition of great faith and hope. But I realized this week that it was not enough. Because I realized that the sense of craziness that comes with realizing one is a heretic—especially if you think you are the only one—is not what is on the minds of the newer people coming here.

I was reminded of Martin Buber's words and Annie Dillard's response in her book *Teaching a Stone to Talk* (so who else is crazy?) Dillard quotes Martin Buber, who says: "The crisis of all primitive mankind comes with the discovery of that which is fundamentally not-holy . . ."[2] Dillard responds, "Now we are no longer primitive; now the whole world seems not-holy. We have drained the light from the boughs in the sacred grove and snuffed it in the high places and along the banks of sacred streams. We as a people have moved from pantheism (God is everywhere and in everything) to pan-atheism (God is nowhere) Silence is not our heritage but our destiny." While I was surprised to find a place that could give a home to a heretic thirty five years ago, today's adventurers through our doors are surprised to find themselves in church at all.

Are *you* crazy? Sitting in a pew. Singing hymns. Listening to a preacher? "What on earth has come over you?" your friends might say. At least your friends back in Chicago or New York, when you tell them you've moved to Dallas and are going to church. Annie Dillard says, "We doused the burning bush and cannot rekindle it; we are lighting matches in vain under every green tree. Did the wind use to cry, and the hills shout forth praise? . . . Now speech has perished from among the lifeless things of earth, and living things say very little to very few."

We're *still* heretics. We're still savoring the quest to know, to pass truth through the fire of our own experience. We're still a congregation of tenacious, and some would say eccentric people. We still struggle with what it means to have a just community, here and in our city and land. This still can be a disquieting place, even after we are relieved to find that we are not alone.

But none of that is so much the issue today, as 'what *is* church.' 'Why come to church'? Is there a magnetic force in society that draws us to church, even against our better judgments? The surprise for many is that we are here at all. I can only give you my best guess. And assure you that you are not crazy to 'try church.'

It seems to me that for perhaps new reasons, people, old and young, have come to the place Rabindranath Tagore wrote of in his collection of Persian Songs. Perhaps we can say that our culture is sensing the truth of what he wrote:

> I thought that my voyage had come to its end at the last limit of my power—that the path before me was closed, that provisions were exhausted and the time come to take shelter in a silent obscurity.
> But I find that . . . when old words die out on the tongue, new melodies break forth from the heart; and where the old tracks are lost, new country is revealed with its wonders.

As crazy as it may seem, church may be the place for new melodies, and new country to be revealed. I can't say that we have the answers here. In fact we make a specialty, I should warn you, of *not* having answers. That part may *drive* you crazy! But for those who may have even an unarticulated sense that "as a single letter of the alphabet, our lives can be meaningless. Or they can be part of a great meaning". Our purpose here is to find our place as part of a great meaning. I won't say that this is the only place it happens. But I will say that if you come, if you plant your life here, and your children's lives. If you who are older make friends of the younger. And you who are starting out, sidle up to the older ones with the intention of learning from them. And if you fill your lungs with air, and sing the melodies of life along with the rest of us. And for this brief hour, give up your need to be autonomous and let yourself be part of this heretical but singing, praying, worshipping congregation. If you take time in the midst of getting and spending and maintaining, to figure out what part you can play in nourishing the soul of our city.

And if you can admit that there might be a silence worth listening to, some truth worth waiting for, some new life worth your yearning—that not only when you show up here, we have to let you in, but in some ultimate way, when you show up for Life, Love embraces you. Then let me tell you, brother and sister, you are not crazy. You are in the right place.

One last word: I took my son to a Unitarian Universalist church for the same reason Anne Lamott did, even when he resisted. I was bigger than he was. At least for a while! When I think back to the people he met, the values he gained, the life he leads now because I made him go to church with me—it has made all the difference. And you will make a difference in children's lives, as well. For all I know, you may be crazy. But if you think you are because your beliefs are not aligned with anything you've heard anywhere. Or if you think you're crazy just getting up and coming to church on a Sunday morning, let me be the first to reassure you. You're very sane. For you are on the path with a whole bunch of other truth-seekers, curious seekers of knowledge, hope, and that voice hidden in the silence some still call God. Welcome. And y'all come back!

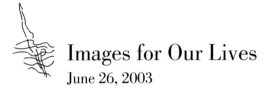

Images for Our Lives
June 26, 2003

This is an essay presented during Ministers' Days at General Assembly in 2003. It is known as a "Berry Street Essay" preached in honor of the Ministers who assembled on Berry Street in Boston each year, before they formed the American Unitarian Association. I wrote this essay as a way to describe my continuing thinking about the religious imagination, which I believe is crucial to the proper role of religion in people's lives. LH

I want to dedicate this essay to the memory of two men who died the same week in March of this year. The first is Harry Scholefield, who was my mentor and friend and partner in the work of articulating a spiritual practice for religious liberals. The second, perhaps less known by many of you is Hardy Sanders, a layperson in my congregation in Dallas—a more passionate and devoted and generous Unitarian Universalist I have not known. These two losses, and what these men stood for, in the midst of so much we have had to bear this year, have weighed heavily on me as I have prepared this essay.

Each one was devoted to our faith. At the same time, Hardy felt that we were frittering away our message with petty diversions. And Harry felt that we, especially we Unitarian Universalist ministers, 'used' poems and wisdom literature, without having lived them. In many ways their lives and concerns shape what I have to say.

Today, I want to talk about imagination. About *religious* imagination, to be more specific. I want to say that we are in a crisis of language—and I believe that we are—because we have forgotten what religious imagination is and does. The purpose of my essay today will be to remind us of the importance of religious imagination in all our varied ministries. In ministry itself.

But first, let me go back to 1971. I was 28 years old, home with my then one-year-old toddler. I had been a teacher and a curriculum consultant in my short career in education prior to that. I was asked by Roy Phillips, the new Minister at Unity Unitarian Church in St. Paul, Minnesota, where I was a member, to join a committee he was forming to rewrite the Sunday school curriculum. He was gathering a group of members, mostly teachers, to talk about what was needed. Mary Anderson was a member of that group of seven. She is Lebanese, was raised a Muslim, is a devoted Unitarian Universalist and helped us broaden our perspective significantly in those days, which now seem so long ago. Roy said that there was a felt need being expressed in the congregation for a religious education that centered on traditional religious themes—an education that would help the children to know themselves as religious people. Would I help?

Needing a project with some challenge in those days, I said, "Yes." It is to a large degree why I stand before you today. Because you can ask people what they believe, and they may tell you something halfway interesting. But if you ask them what should be taught to their children, you quickly get down to basics. We were about the gritty and difficult duty of deciding what would be taught our children, and how and why. The curriculum was called *Images for Our Lives.*

That work, which took up four years of our lives, was long ago and far away. But I bring it up because I learned two important points that apply to what I want to say today.

The first was our decision always to look for the "religious existential dimension" of the story we were teaching, whether the story was from the Judeo-Christian tradition (as we called it in those days), or from our own Unitarian Universalist tradition, or from other world religions. We actually devised a chart. It was called "Three Ways of Interpreting a Story". The first was the "Literal, Popular, Fundamentalist interpretation." The second was the "Rational, Critical, Historical interpretation." And the third was the "Religious, Existential, Spiritual Interpretation."

I was familiar with the first one. I had been raised a fundamentalist. I knew my Bible, and I knew the literal interpretations of the story. And to some degree, we were familiar with the rational, critical, historical interpretations. Although Roy recounted once that he had been taught in his Unitarian Sunday School, in an *attempt* at a rational interpretation, that when it came to the story of Jesus walking on water, Jesus had really walked on sandbars.

We had some sense of the new thought that had brought about Biblical criticism, and it had more substance than sandbars, we knew. So we made a place in our chart for such interpretations.

It was the third category that most interested us, though. The Religious, Existential, Spiritual interpretation. I'm not sure where that phrase came from. It wasn't tied to Existentialism *per se.* Roy said he used the dictionary definition at first: "grounded in existence or the experience of existence." But after much discussion we decided that the "Religious Existential Dimension" of each story was to be the center of our work. We would try to find the part of each story that would allow the children to "take the story as an image of their own experience of life."

For example, the Noah story. The story of Noah became less a story about a god who wanted to start things over, and more an incredible image of a tiny boat, built to specifications, but oh so small in that huge sea, and of Noah, who had been so faithful, left for five months with no horizon, no contact, with nothing happening. That was something we could resonate with. And if our children couldn't at the time, at least they would have it as a container for their life-experience in the future.

At some point, we thought, if one of our children was in a life situation with no shore in sight, as if forgotten by their Mamas and their Papas, and even by God, we wanted them to remember Noah. We wanted them to be connected in a deep way to all those others who had felt forgotten until they sent out a dove and it returned with an olive branch—all those others who had to wait so long for hope to return.

That is why we called it "Images for our Lives." Every story we presented, whether Noah or Emerson or Kisogatami, was considered in its Religious Existential Dimension: as an image of existence, with imagination, with the recall of an image with which our children could associate their life experiences.

Which brings me to the second point I learned while working on that curriculum. We called it the "piñata effect." At one of our weekly meetings, we were going over a lesson. It was a good lesson educationally. The author was quite sophisticated in the development of curriculum, and had created an interesting and compelling lesson with a piñata at the center. And who among us hasn't had a piñata at some church event or other.

When we asked her what the "religious existential dimension" of the piñata lesson was, she couldn't name it. It was interesting culturally, the children would have a great time, it might be group building, but it did not point to anything beyond itself, it could not be "grounded in the experience of existence", at least in the imaginative way we were working. It was simply interesting. She agreed to throw the lesson out.

From then on, whenever we were, however brilliantly, creating curriculum that strayed from our purpose of nurturing the religious existential and spiritual dimension of our material, we simply said "piñata" and out it went.

To this day, when I am writing a sermon, or preparing a lesson, the word "piñata" will rise up in my consciousness, and I will realize that no matter how eloquent, no matter how clever, it is not doing what I should be doing—which is to speak to the depth of human experience.

Today I want to say that one of the reasons we are having a crisis of language among ourselves, is because we haven't said "piñata" enough. It is because we have been charmed, sometimes by the sound of our own voices, sometimes by the brilliance of our own minds, speaking eloquently about this or that, but forgetting the foundation of our work in the world—the religious existential dimension of life. The communication from person to person and generation to generation of a kind of truth that is based on the reality, as Bernard Meland once said," that we live more deeply than we think."[1]

If the Religious Existential Reality is "grounded in the experience of existence", and "we live more deeply than we think", then we had better find ways to say that which is deeper than we can speak.

Now, I am keenly aware of my audience here today. Most of you are off the scale when it comes to our verbal abilities—after all, didn't the Wall Street Journal recently tell us that the young people in our churches score the highest on the SAT's in the nation? We who are the leaders of perhaps the most educated group in the country—though we're embarrassed to admit it—so often forget what we know when it comes to religious language. And we forget that it is our job to teach our congregations what we know.

I recently spoke to our Adult Sunday School Class in Dallas on the topic "Why I am not a Theist". They packed the room to hear what I had to say, because of course they thought I was. Why did they think I was a Theist? Because I use the word God. Because I pray in the midst of the worship service. I was embarrassed a bit myself, to find that I had failed to make the distinction that the use of metaphors and poetry and scripture has to do with religious imagination, and not with one theological category or another. We had a lively and productive discussion that day, as I spoke, as I am today, about religious language, and how it communicates the depths of experience, and that it isn't always what it seems.

I remember when the Principles and Purposes were being formulated in meetings years ago all across our continent. Peter Fleck, of beloved memory, who was on the committee to synthesize those formulations, said that he had noticed a curious thing. When he asked individual Unitarian Universalists where they stood theologically, he said, "They would juxtapose two seemingly opposite theological categories together. Like Christian-Humanist, or Agnostic-Christian, or Rational-Mystic, refusing to align themselves with one distinct theology." Peter was puzzled by this.

I now think it was the beginning of our attempts to extricate ourselves from the hard theological boundaries within which we had closed ourselves off from one another and from our experience of religious imagination, and of deep reality.

When I arrived at Theological School, I found there were other languages of currency, other ways we were extricating ourselves from the boundaries of theological language and categories. These languages were mainly psychological and political: the psychological to give meaning, and the political to give purpose. We learned the language of ethical discourse, and of course the languages of various theologies, as well. But the real categories of discussion among us were psychological and political. Gone were the earlier days of humanist/theist debates. In their place were struggles to integrate our ministries with the problems of the world and the pathologies of our lives.

I was later to be intrigued by Harry Scholefield's story of having undergone several years of Freudian Analysis in Philadelphia. He had been invited into the Psychoanalytic Institute, in a special program for people who were professionals in areas other than psychology. He ended up immersing himself in analysis. He told the story of the importance of his analysis to his ministry in a Berry Street Essay in 1962: "Motivation in the Ministry."[2] Harry could also speak the language of the political life of his times. He was a well known Peace and Fair Housing activist in San Francisco, where he was minister for the largest portion of his career.

I came, during my theological years and afterward, to deeply respect the power of psychological and political thought and action and language in the shaping of who we are and what we are to do in the world.

And I also came to understand that pathology could not be the only focus for our inner work, and saw too many political activists who burned out because their activism was not grounded. There was something else that was needed to deepen our meaning and purpose. That something else was the language of religious imagination.

The problem with language is that those words, those simple individual words are slippery little devils. They don't stay put.

I remember my shock, as a junior high school student, when I used the word "queer" thinking it meant "odd" and discovering to my dismay that it was a pejorative label used to mean a homosexual. I was horrified! Partly because I was in junior high school. Partly because I didn't mean what people thought I meant. But I was most horrified that the word didn't mean what I thought it did.

Until that point I had assumed that words meant what they meant—that words stood still. They stood firm against all the vicissitudes of life. And in that moment, my faith in language was shaken. Words could add meaning, they could change meaning, they could turn on you. I was shocked. (I should also add that at that time in my life I was a Religious Fundamentalist, as well. It may have been that more than my faith in *words* was shaken that day.)

And then I was to discover that the word, for example "God", could become the victim of what Whitehead called "misplaced concreteness".[3] Words, over time, could lose their rich, metaphorical, living depth, and become concrete—rigidified and lifeless. The imaginative vitality could ebb away. The *word* "God" could die.

So if words don't stand still, if they are subject, over time, to misplaced concreteness; if they don't necessarily represent one theology or another; if they are inadequate, even when they serve political and psychological purposes and give us some meaning and purpose; if they need to point to the depths of lived experience, the religious existential dimension of life; if we live more deeply than we can think; if we are currently in a crisis of language (which I believe we are); if we are truly to minister in the fields of human need; what will save us from ourselves?

My answer is Poetry.

Now, if that answer disappoints you, I will only ask that you stick with me. If verbal though we all are, poetry was an add-on in high school, a linguistic burden in college, and another complex system of signs and symbols to learn in graduate school—let me quickly explain that by poetry I mean all words and phrases, even whole narrative stories that point beyond themselves to the depth of human experience. I believe that poetry is scripture. I believe that scripture is poetry. I believe that poetry is the way deep truth is transmitted person-to-person and generation-to-generation. I believe that when Emily Dickinson said, "Tell the truth/but tell it slant",[3] she was speaking of metaphorical truth, the poetic truth that nourishes the heart, and opens the mind, and communicates to the depths. By poetry, I mean the products of the religious imagination.

First, let me say that I am keenly aware that there are many products of the imagination that are not centered in words. So if poetry seems an extraordinarily limited focus for all the possibilities of metaphorical truth that can communicate deeply—I will admit it is. But again, I want to remember where I am, and who we are, and what we do week after week after week. I know there are many different ministries represented here; and I hope you'll bear with me if I narrow my scope and talk about words and their uses between and among us, acknowledging that music and art and even the silences of the soul are more profound than I could convey today. But speaking I am, and so we're going for Religious Imagination, the verbal expression of the depth of human experience.

Second, let me say that by Religious Imagination, I am not speaking only of the products of the imagination that have explicit religious references.

Consider Philip Booth's wonderful poem, *First Lesson*, about teaching his daughter to swim:

Lie back, daughter, let your head
be tipped back in the cup of my hand.
Gently, and I will hold you. Spread
your arms wide, lie out on the stream
and look high at the gulls. A dead-
man's float is face down. You will dive
and swim soon enough where this tidewater
ebbs to the sea. Daughter, believe
me, when you tire on the long thrash
to your island, lie up, and survive.
As you float now, where I held you
and let go, remember when fear
cramps your heart what I told you:
lie gently and wide to the light-year
stars, lie back, and the sea will hold you.[4]

This poem has *not one* traditional religious word in it. And yet it associates to deep realities beyond itself and across generations of human experience.

For a time I thought this would be enough. There are certainly enough images and stories out there to take us to the heights and depths of human experience without having to bother with traditional religious language. These poems and narratives would have to fulfill certain criteria, of course. They would have to take on associative meeting, they would have to break concrete meanings open, they would have to be relational, they would have to name experience in a way that takes us beyond ourselves, and even beyond the experience itself. Surely there is enough spoken and written in the literature of humankind to be able to speak to human experience without having to evoke a God, or think about Prayer, or use any of the words that have specifically religious associative meanings—those meanings that are so encumbered as to be almost impossible to use. Or so it seemed to me at the time.

First Lesson should be enough. But then I heard a simple explanation about a Russian Orthodox Icon. The Priest explained that the value given the icon was in its ability to teach the people who sat with it. "They didn't analyze it. It taught them," he said. ("Not very American," he added.) Being from a more plain tradition, I never pursued iconography, and have always worried about idolatry, but that simple explanation changed how I thought about the traditional words of Western religion. I couldn't drop them. They had evoked too much for too many people, over too long a time, and I needed to stay connected to the human struggles, the human understandings they represented, if only to inform my own. The word "God" might have become concretized. The *word* "God" might even have died. But I could not ignore all that it represented before it passed into a state of rigor mortis.

Suzanne Langer, in her book *Philosophy in a New Key*, was also helpful on this point. She says,

> "This tendency is comprehensible enough if we consider the preeminence with which a named element holds the kaleidoscopic flow of sheer sense and feeling. For as soon as an object is denoted, it can be held, so that anything else that is experienced at the same time, instead of crowding it out, is experienced with it, in contrast or in unison or in some other way . . . A word fixes something in experience, and makes it the nucleus of memory, an available conception. Other impressions group themselves round the denoted thing and are associatively recalled when it is named."[6]

Who was I to drop these words that had meant so much to our very own spiritual ancestors, as well as generations of human seekers, even if the associations might be complex? And perhaps the word "God" wasn't as dead as I had thought.

Interestingly, I remembered, too, that Harry Scholefield had called his Freudian analysis, "The relentless practice of association." He said that whatever associated to the topic at hand in analysis, had to be faced. It was a difficult practice, he said. And one that took years fully to embrace.

Later in his life, Harry was to move his "relentless practice of association" into his meditative times, waiting for the words of poets and scribes to associate with each other, and with his lived experiences. "Sometimes," he said, "Walt (that would be Walt Whitman) would arrive, and have a comment or two, and then Emily (that would be Emily Dickinson) would join in." And he said, "Sometimes I had a sense of Presence, of being encompassed about by something larger than I was in those moments, perhaps through the word of a Psalmist, and we would all have a conversation."

Language is a relational system, Suzanne Langer says. A word, especially one of depth of experience, has many associations, and our job is to be open to those associations, because they take us deeper than we can think. Because we are not observers. We are participating in the conversation with our very lives.

The best example I know of this is this poem by Anne Sexton *The Rowing Endeth*:

> I'm mooring my rowboat
> at the dock of the island called God.
> This dock is made in the shape of a fish
> and there are many boats moored
> at many different docks.
> "It's okay," I say to myself,
> with blisters that broke and healed
> and broke and healed—
> saving themselves over and over.
> And salt sticking to my face and arms like
> a glue-skin pocked with grains of tapioca.
> I empty myself from my wooden boat
> and onto the flesh of The Island.
>
> "On with it!" He says and thus
> we squat on the rocks by the sea
> and play—can it be true—
> a game of poker.
> He calls me.
> I win because I hold a royal straight flush.
> He wins because He holds five aces.
> A wild card had been announced
> but I had not heard it

being in such a state of awe
when He took out the cards and dealt.
As he plunks down His five aces
and I sit grinning at my royal flush,
He starts to laugh,
the laughter rolling like a hoop out of His mouth
and into mine,
and such laughter that He doubles right over me
laughing a Rejoice-Chorus at our two triumphs.
Then I laugh, the fishy dock laughs
the sea laughs. The Island laughs.
The Absurd laughs.

Dearest dealer,
I with my royal straight flush,
love you so for your wild card,
that untamable, eternal, gut-driven ha-ha
and lucky love.[7]

I didn't play cards when I was a Fundamentalist, and for sure God didn't! The God I knew, even with all *His* spoken and unspoken associations, concretized as *He* was, is broken open into a dealer who deals, not the plan for my life, but a wild card—untamable, eternal, gut-driven *ha-ha* and lucky love. How could I not welcome such an intrusion into my solidified vision?

If, as Langer asserts, language is a relational system, with associations forming themselves around a more concretized concept, then it is *hubris* for us to believe that we can cut out some words, and put others on the back burner—for they will find their way back into consciousness, often in surprising ways. As Harry used to say, "They just put up a hand, saying, Wait, I have something to say." What we need to do then is to break open these concretized words, to juxtapose them with words that create cognitive dissonance. For it is in the spaces between the juxtapositions that new associations are created.

The first inkling I had of that was when we began to use the pronoun "She" for "God". When they heard those words for the first time, people laughed nervously, you might not have been there, but it is true. People laughed. It was so strange. So odd.

The idea that metaphors that have suffered "misplaced concreteness" can be brought to life by simply juxtaposing them in surprising ways, is almost too simple. It creates a cognitive dissonance in the listener that breaks them open—not to new *definitions* of God, or whatever element of mystery you are attempting to point toward, but to a small portion of reality that they have experienced. Remember, we're talking about the religious existential dimension of life, not definitions. We're talking about the products of the imagination here. We're pointing, not positing.

I want to talk about another element of our linguistic crisis: that is the language of yearning. It's not only that, but let's start there. Early in my ministry I began to question why people were coming to see me. The problems and issues they brought into my study were posed in psychological terms. I knew that there were enough therapists in town to cover the needs of my whole congregation. "Why were they coming to me?" I asked. Perhaps, I told myself, it was because I was a minister. They didn't have the language to speak it, but they had the depth to feel it. They needed *spiritual* counsel. One day, feeling rather bold, I asked a person who was in my office if she had prayed about her situation. Without hesitation, she said, "Yes. I feel like a child again, but I can't help myself."

It gave me some traction, some place to minister. "Shall we pray about it now?" I asked, not sure of what I would say. She said "yes" and we did.

I can't say it was transformative for her. Although I had the keen sense that, at some level, she expected that is what we would do. But I will say that it changed my understanding about why people were coming to me. It was because I was a minister! They expected me to ask them about things like prayer. They expected me to take them somewhere beyond that childhood version of prayer they remembered.

I have learned always to ask. I remember once visiting a woman who did not have long to live. She was a firm skeptic. I knew that. But I thought, perhaps, in this tender moment, she might want her minister to pray her through. I asked, "Would you like me to pray?" She was so forceful in her "no" that I actually thought I might have given her a renewed reason to live!

So I want you to know that I'm not advocating one path, or one way. These are products of the imagination, not definitions of ministerial methods. With that caveat, I will say that I am convinced that our congregations need a vocabulary of yearning. And that is prayer. They need an opportunity to name their relationship with Life in relational words—in poetry, in metaphor. They need to pray.

I was fortunate that when I went to Dallas that prayer was already part of the service. Slowly, I introduced relational words. Slowly I directed the prayer to "God of many names, and mystery beyond all our naming . . ." Slowly I began to ask for help and comfort and wisdom and strength. Slowly I began to name individuals who needed our prayer, and with whom we were celebrating. I gave thanks for new babies, and grieved over lost loved ones—naming fathers and mothers, and sisters and brothers who had died. I prayed our inadequacy to face the pain of our days. This is not a rational posit to a responding deity. It is not a posture of groveling. It is an expression of our yearning, our grief, our gratitude. It has become an expression of our congregation as a whole.

Every once in awhile someone asks me "Who" I think I'm praying to . . . I recall the good advice from Alcoholic Anonymous 12 step programs. "Just take care of your side of the street" that sage wisdom goes. And that's what I do with prayer. I take care of my side of the street, with my gratitude and amazement and praise, and fear and anger and hurt. And as well the side of the street that my congregation is on. I figure the other side of the street can take care of itself and we can save the theological discussions for later.

I was lucky enough to inherit from Robert Raible's ministry in my Dallas church, the closing to the prayer, which I commend to you. People have said that they wept when they first heard these words:

> We pray in the names of all those, known and unknown, present
> and absent, remembered and forgotten. We pray in the names of all
> the helpers of humankind.

This is language that opens up rather than shutting off.

This is language that points beyond rather than positing definitions.

This is language that connects us with the yearning of humankind, of all sorts and kinds, rather than setting us apart as literal in our rejection, closed in our disdain, set apart in our determination to reject language that will not imagine anything beyond what we see and know. Remember, we do live more deeply than we think. We must, as religious leaders, point through our thinking, connecting to the depths of life, where our people live.

I once was taken with the idea put forth by two therapists about the importance of having a "richness of model." They said that when people came with this or that difficulty, they found that their ability to overcome their problems was largely determined by their "richness of model." If they had a thin model of life and its possibilities, they would have little probability of finding new ways of living that would improve their relationships. If their model of life was varied and open, with many possibilities envisioned, they would have a much higher probability of adapting to new ways of being.[8]

"What is it," we might ask, "that would contribute to a person's 'richness of model?'" I wouldn't want to limit such a discussion among us—but I am convinced that before education, before life experience, before even the quality of our relationships that have brought us along—I would say, one of the possible contributing factors to a person's 'richness of model' is religious imagination.

For that is where we name our experience, that is where we forge our relationship to what is, that is where we know who we are, what we are living for, and where our yearning is. For what is the poetic, but an attempt to name experience in a relational way? I can hear Walt (that would be Whitman) saying:

You air that serves me with breath to speak!
You objects that call from diffusion and give
    them shape!
You light that wraps me and all things in delicate equable
    showers
You paths worn in the irregular hollows by the roadsides!
I believe you are latent with unseen existences, you are so
    dear to me.[9]

Religious imagination opens us to an encompassing "You" of life that takes on a complexity of relationship (a richness of model) we can nurture and cultivate, for ourselves, and for those with whom we minister.

But then there is Harry Scholefield raising a hand and saying, "Wait, I have something to say. This isn't about preaching, or counseling, or the various ways we speak in our ministries—it is about our own depth as ministers. It is about living into the language of *our* ministries."

"How's *your* meditative life," he would ask me. "You talk about "Images for Our Lives". You mean "Images for *Our* Lives". Yours and mine. For how can we speak to the depths, if we are living in the shallows of busyness, where more than a few of us abide.

Late in Harry's ministry he significantly changed the way he worked, trying to have his ministry arise more from the depths of his experience, than from the demands of the moment. He had always memorized poetry, and so he increasingly turned to the poetry he had memorized as a kind of mantra for meditation. He said that the more he leaned into wisdom words from scripture and poets, and even such prose as the Gettysburg Address and Lincoln's Second Inaugural—the more he sat with those words, the more they began to associate—with other poems, with experiences in his life, with creative realities entering into the conversation.

What Langer had said about the associative properties of language suddenly became substantive in a person whose life and practice I could see. Here was a man who might have called himself a Religious Humanist. He certainly wasn't a Christian, or a Theist. He worried over the use of the word God—and yet found solace in the 139th Psalm, found grounding for his activism in the words of the Prophets, especially Amos, and found his inner life peopled with Rumi and Rilke.

Here was Associative Devotional Practice: juxtaposing images in a sermon, or using the words God/she to break open the concretizing tendency of language and refresh meaning, are less tools of the trade, and more sources for the soul—certainly where our ministries have to originate if we are to do any good. Memorizing scripture and poetry and prose has become a spiritual practice for me, and a way into the spiritual lives of the very real people with whom I minister.

In other words, juxtaposing words and images began to arise from within my own being, out of my own spiritual practice ("having their own conversation," Harry might have said) but to my mind, creating the kind of cognitive dissonances that keeps my life open and fresh.

Some of us have "found" poetry. We certainly have enough inspirational writing to keep us going for the next century. But at the end of the poem with which we begin a board or program council meeting—when we all pause for an appropriately thoughtful moment before plunging into the business of the evening—at that moment, where is the living word? Where is the word of our lives, of our hearts? Harry was right. It's where we live. And unless our lives are expressed in those words of inspiration—they will go the way of all concretized words, into the hardened blocks of calcified religion, of no living use or help in the pains and joys of our lives.

I don't know about your congregation, but mine has within it the full range of human joy and despair. I learned in my years at a church in a University town, that the people didn't come to church to have an Adjunct to the University. They came to church to nourish their spiritual natures, to give voice to their hopes and their despair, to speak depth to depth with others, finding their natures beyond psychological language, and their purpose beyond political categories—to find meaning, purpose, and understanding in the religious language of the centuries, of necessity broken open yet one more time through association, through cognitive dissonance, through the naming of common yearnings and hopes, as well as failures. Challenging dogma wherever it occurs, in others and in ourselves. And taking religious language back from the fundamentalists, from the literalists who claim it as if it had always been their own. Seeing poetry and metaphor and some amazing examples of prose that serve as a scripture for our time, as much as the scriptures which have spoken to generations before us, before they were calcified and solidified by the process of concretization and allowed to die.

We not only need to invite poets into the rooms of our hearts, but we need to invite our spiritual ancestors as well. They are raising a hand or two, wanting to be heard. If we say, "We'll listen but don't use any words that have become solidified in the meantime, no matter how fulsome they were for you"—we will have cut ourselves off, not only from our spiritual DNA, but also from one part of the conversation that we desperately need to have.

Our President has called us to a language of reverence. We need a language of reverence. We need a language of forgiveness. We need a language of reconciliation. A language of hope. A language that gives voice to despair. To name a few. That language for centuries, and in countless cultures has been metaphorical, it has pointed beyond itself to something much deeper than it could name. It is our turn to keep such language alive, hold it to our hearts, and speak to the depths of those who so desperately need our good word.

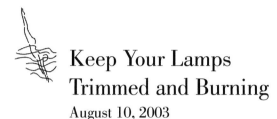

Keep Your Lamps
Trimmed and Burning
August 10, 2003

The best thing about these biblical stories is that they can still be mined for depth. It was astounding to me when I realized this story wasn't about taking care of contingencies. I can't say that I gave up list-making and task-fulfilling on the spot. But it did help me see beyond the usual interpretations of the story, and even beyond the problem of ten maidens waiting for one bridegroom, to understand it as a deep metaphor of spiritual preparation for the gifts of life. LH

Matthew 25:14-30

Then the kingdom of heaven shall be compared to ten maidens who took their lamps and went to meet the bridegroom.

Five of them were foolish, and five were wise.

For when the foolish took their lamps, they took no oil with them; but the wise took flasks of oil with their lamps.

As the bridegroom was delayed, they all slumbered and slept.

But at midnight there was a cry, 'Behold, the bridegroom! Come out to meet him.'

Then all those maidens rose and trimmed their lamps. And the foolish said to the wise,

'Give us some of your oil, for our lamps are going out.'

But the wise replied, 'Perhaps there will not be enough for us and for you; go rather to the dealers and buy for yourselves.'

And while they went to buy, the bridegroom came, and those who were ready went in with him to the marriage feast; and the door was shut.

Afterward the other maidens came also, saying, 'Lord, lord, open to us.'

But he replied, 'Truly, I say to you, I do not know you.'

Watch therefore, for you know neither the day nor the hour.

Joy from <u>The Book of Qualities</u>
By J. Ruth Gendler

Joy drinks pure water. She has sat with the dying and attended many births. She denies nothing. She is in love with life, all of it, the sun and the rain and the rainbow. She rides horses at Half Moon Bay under the October moon. She climbs mountains. She sings in the hills. She jumps from the hot spring to the cold stream without hesitation.

Although Joy is spontaneous, she is immensely patient. She does not need to rush. She knows that there are obstacles on every path and that every moment is the perfect moment. She is not concerned with success or failure or how to make things permanent.

At times Joy is elusive—she seems to disappear even as we approach her. I see her standing on a ridge covered with oak trees, and suddenly the distance between us feels enormous. I am overwhelmed and wonder if the effort to reach her is worth it. Yet, she waits for us. Her desire to walk with us is as great as our longing to accompany her.[1]

This is the sermon that I wish I had heard when I was a child. If you heard sermons about this passage, I'll be willing to wager that you will wish you had heard this sermon before now too. If you've never heard the story then you may be wondering why we would bother with a First Century story about maidens and lamps. If that's the case, then I say, "Listen up. It's in the culture, it's in the air. You need to know what it's about—if only to impress your friends next week when you tell them the significance of this biblical story. The friends and relatives that think you don't go to a real church."

Of course, the real reason you need to know about the ten maidens and the lamps is because it has deep truth in it. I follow the basic premise that a story over 2000 years old shouldn't be dismissed out of hand. Even if it takes a little digging to get to the heart of it.

Biblical scholars tell us that this story is built around First Century Palestinian wedding customs. It is one of several stories about the end times, set in the book of Matthew as if it is a story Jesus told himself. The wait for Jesus had already been longer than they had thought, and so it is easy to see why stories about that wait might be inserted here for the followers of Jesus who believed that, after his Crucifixion and Resurrection, he would come back to get them. "Be ready" would be a good teaching for a people who thought Jesus should have already come back for them.

As I said earlier, this story had a significant impact on me as a Fundamentalist. Both in its literal sense, and in its metaphorical sense. You can imagine the power such a story would have on a little girl, especially of my generation or earlier. Perhaps even now on little girls when it is told literally. *I* would be ready when *my* Groom arrived. And *I* would be ready when Jesus came to take believers to heaven with him. Jesus and the husband God had chosen for me were pretty mixed together in those days. *I* would wait.

In those days, childhood seemed to be a continual pattern of waiting. Waiting for school to start. Waiting for school to end. Waiting to go to the circus. Waiting to get a TV (we were definitely not the first ones on our block to have one.) Waiting to watch TV (it only came on after 5:00 p.m. at my house). Waiting to get a two wheel bicycle. Waiting to grow up!

"Ten maidens took their lamps to wait for the bridegroom." And the bridegroom "tarried", the story says. There is usually not much emphasis put on this part of the story, at least in its traditional sense.

This would definitely be a red flag today. A bridegroom who shows up for his own wedding so late it's midnight, and many of the people who are waiting for him have fallen asleep? *Definitely* a red flag! And it should have been even for those who were waiting for Jesus to come for them. We wonder, don't we, about the people who sell everything and go stand on a hilltop, waiting for Jesus on a certain date and at a certain time. What happens to them when nothing happens? I'm sure they adjust. But this story is an interesting portent for Christians who are too sure they know how things will happen in relation to Jesus' second coming. At least so far we know He's late. It's not happening when we thought it would.

It usually takes time and experience to realize that things don't usually happen when we think they should. That everything takes a lot longer than we expect. Such tenacity is a very important human quality to add to any measure of hope we may have. So the ten maidens—whether metaphorically or in some sense of the reality of our own lives—sit down to wait. It's late. Nothing's happening. And soon they slowly drift off to sleep.

There doesn't seem to be any problem with that. Waiting can be simply . . . waiting. And the maidens are not brought into any judgment about their slumber. The problem is that some of them did not prepare for this contingency. They didn't expect they would have to wait. They certainly didn't think they would have to wait so long.

I think I can assume that most of us are not waiting for Jesus' return. And I think I can also assume that we have had the experience of expecting certain things that have not arrived.

My son's mother—and father-in-law are Austrians who grew up during World War II. As young adults they threw themselves into *Fokolare*, an international movement which promotes peace—at home, in their villages, and internationally. It grew out of their Catholic faith, but included people especially from Japan, Germany, Austria, and Italy. They aspired to prevent the causes of war at the core of people's lives. A testament to their openness came when their daughter returned from a short term job in the United States with an American Unitarian Universalist boyfriend. They welcomed him and me and our family without hesitation.

Now, after a lifetime of working in some very good and basic ways to create connections between people, they were shocked by 911, and perhaps even more so by our actions in Iraq. They remain discouraged about the lack of peace between Israel and the Palestinians and wonder if peace is possible. I know they have contemporaries here today who wonder the same thing. Who wait. And it all takes so much longer than anyone could imagine. It seems impossible at times.

But if not world peace, there are plenty of other things we wait for. We could come up with at least 100 things—right now, even in this culture of immediate gratification—100 things we are waiting for. I know a couple of mothers who are really ready for their babies to arrive. There are at least two weddings being planned by couples in our congregation. There are some long difficult declines—with death on the horizon—of loved ones. There is a waiting for death among us.

And then there is this question of having enough oil for our lamps to make it through. It seems to always take longer than we think it will. At least that is my experience. And then, after waiting, there is the question of being prepared. Remember, only five of the maidens came prepared with extra oil in case the bridegroom was late. At midnight the cry went out, "The bridegroom cometh" and the young women, who had been slumbering, awakened and went out to meet him. The five who had no extra oil, could not relight their lamps. Commentaries on this story say that weddings in that time were so significant that study in the temple ceased, and most activities were suspended while the feast took place. So, it is feasible that in that party-atmosphere there were places to buy oil at midnight.

I heard years ago that in the Talmud it says that if a wedding procession and a funeral cortege meet, the wedding procession passes first. It is a good rule of thumb. The celebration of life precedes the marking of death. I have had occasion in my ministry to share that simple principle when life's demands converge at difficult times. In this case, the story points to the celebration surpassing everything else. The five maidens who had not brought extra oil went to find some to buy. So the story turns from "waiting" to "having made contingency plans".

Here's a rhetorical question: I wonder how many of us feel we are *constantly* "getting ready". We who thought the assignments would end once we got out of school! Getting ready for events. Getting our family ready for school, for a trip, a visit. Getting our houses ready for guests, getting meals ready to be eaten. Getting ready for a presentation at work. Getting ready. Getting ready.

In the story, those were the wise ones—the ones who were prepared. They had extra oil. The foolish ones were the ones who had to go out at midnight to find an open shop where perhaps they could buy some. You've seen them. The man walking down the street with a red plastic gasoline container in his hand. "How could that happen?" we ask ourselves as we drive by. "How could he run out of gas?" Foolish one. So it has been centuries that we have been labeling the unprepared, "foolish."

But here's the part I wish I had heard long ago, when I was taught this story. Here's the part that I see now that I couldn't see then: the five young women who had to go out to find oil for their lamps were unprepared for *joy*.

All my life I have thought that being prepared meant having all the details attended to. All the tasks finished. Most of us would think that. After all, the food does have to be put on the table, the suitcases do have to be packed with clean clothes, the travel arrangements must be made. These are all tasks. These are all things to be ticked off a list before something can happen.

But this metaphor, this story of preparedness—deep in the consciousness of most of western culture, whether we know it or not—is *not* about getting the list accomplished. The wisdom of the young women who were prepared, if we see this story not as doctrine about the second coming, and not as literal representation of tasks at hand—but as deep metaphor about life—is about keeping our lamps burning, and being prepared for the emergency of joy.

How do we prepare for joy? I don't think going out at midnight to buy more oil for our lamps will do it. It's not a task. It's not even a self-help's book worth. How does one prepare for the possibility, even the emergency of joy? In J. Ruth Gendler's sweet book on *Qualities* she personifies Joy as someone who is spontaneous, but also "immensely patient". The wise young women in the biblical story neither get ahead of themselves with impatience, nor behind themselves with frustration. They know how to wait. So if you're a list-maker, under Joy, I'd put down, "Learn to wait." You'd probably have to rearrange your life a bit to do that, but it's not a bad idea. Joy has sat with the dying, and attended many births. I've sat with the dying. I haven't attended many births, except my own and the birth of my son. Both of those times I was rather distracted! But I think you know my point. Because they are connected—birth and death. Very much part of the same process. And most of the time, both take longer than one would wish. There is a strange kind of waiting at each end of our lives. And there is joy in coming to know that connection.

"Joy jumps from hot spring to the cold stream without hesitation." I think that's asking a lot. I knew some Swedes in Minnesota who spoke longingly of the days when they would sit in a Sauna and then jump into the snow. But I thought that a little extreme. And yet, there are days when life gives me vertigo. When the juxtaposition of joys and sorrows is so intense I'm not sure I can bear it. It is the peculiar lot of ministry, but it comes to everyone. This wind shear of events that pull at our grief and our ecstasy at the same time. Some today call it "bandwidth"—tolerating complexity in the midst of real time living. That tolerance can make room for joy.

I know there are some churches that go for joy without owning the tragic dimension of life. I cannot preach avoidance of the very real tragedy we see all around us. But if tragedy is all we see, than we are no different. Better to cultivate the ability to jump from the hot spring to the cold stream without hesitation. To cultivate a bandwidth of response to all of life, not one narrow band or another. So number two on the Joy list is to *broaden your bandwidth to include joy when it appears.*

Joy, according to Ms. Gendler, is not concerned with success or failure or how to make things permanent. Easy for her to say! But, having failed, and having succeeded, and having tried to make things permanent, I have to say she's right. Perhaps that's one item for the list that can't be added until one has done all three. Because this is not an invitation to cease to care, or to cease to make commitments. For Joy is right there in the midst of the successes and failures and commitments. But Joy doesn't care which it is—success or failure, that is. Success brings a flush of happiness; failure brings its sense of shame. Trying to make things as they are, permanent, brings its own kind of frustration. But Joy is not concerned with any of it. So, if you have been there, at both edges, and working hard in the middle to nail it down, then you can put on your list number three: *Joy doesn't get bothered about success or failure or permanence.*

Joy is elusive, Gendler says. Yes. But I wished I'd known that Joy wasn't all *that* elusive. I wished I'd known long ago, when I first heard the story of the virgins who waited for the bridegroom, and who were or weren't prepared, that it had nothing to do with being alert to every possible contingency. That it had nothing to do with taking care of details. That it actually had nothing to do with bridegrooms. But it had *everything* to do with being ready to welcome Joy.

You Do Not Have To Be Good
February 29, 2004

This poem by Mary Oliver is one of my favorites. I say it to myself when I am driving, and at other intervals in the day. You just have to find your place 'in the family of things.' It's simple enough, it could take a lifetime. LH

Wild Geese
By Mary Oliver

> You do not have to be good.
> You do not have to walk on your knees
> for a hundred miles through the desert, repenting.
> You only have to let the soft animal of your body
>   love what it loves.
> Tell me about despair, yours, and I will tell you mine.
> Meanwhile the world goes on.
> Meanwhile the sun and the clear pebbles of the rain
> are moving across the landscapes,
> over the prairies and the deep trees,
> the mountains and the rivers.
> Meanwhile the wild geese, high in the clean blue air,
> are heading home again.
> Whoever you are, no matter how lonely,
> the world offers itself to your imagination,
> calls to you like the wild geese, harsh and exciting—
> over and over announcing your place
> in the family of things.[1]

I've wanted to say this for a long time from this pulpit: "You do not have to be good." Partly because I never heard it in my church growing up. Partly because I imagine it's not said much in churches, even today. Partly because I think I know who you are. That hearing those words will not send you off into a frenzy of wrongdoing, but in fact may be words of liberation. Words that need to be heard in a time when our Pilgrim/Puritan heritage, mixed with some cultural pridefulness, has compelled us to work so hard at "being good."

Someone said to me this week that they thought the church existed to help us be better people. And I agree. But today, I want to join Mary Oliver and say, "You do not have to be good."

Let's just try this on for the next few minutes. All those little challenges you give yourself to be a better person, to improve yourself, to overcome your shortcomings. From turning down that second piece of pie to making the world a better place. For the next few minutes, let it all go. Let that gnawing sense that you are not doing enough go. Let your need to take care of situations and people go. Let your need to 'be on top of things' go. You can pick all that up at the door after the service, but for now, let it go. "You do not have to be good. You do not have to walk on your knees for a hundred miles through the desert, repenting."

Now, to be fair, I will tell you that I grew up as a Fundamentalist Baptist. And though there is a lot of love in that faith, in my particular version of Fundamentalism there was also a lot of hell and brimstone preaching. Repentance was high on the list. As a child, believing I was so sinful, I found it hard to be human.

I know that my experience was not everyone's experience, but I think enough of us got that message in one way or another that it's important to say "You do not have to be good" from this pulpit today. As a corrective to all the little ways we deny our humanity, stifle our creativity, take responsibility for much more than is ours, and in general strive to be something we aren't, all in the name of "goodness".

It is important to say "You do not have to be good" as a corrective to the doctrine of original sin, which seems to be everywhere this week with the release of the movie "The Passion of Christ." The doctrine that we all killed the Christ is again on the ascendancy. It is important to know that God doesn't need to allow his son to be killed so that we can be forgiven for being human. It's an interesting story in the history of religions, but not one to rest at the center of who we are, and how we are to be in the world. "You do not have to walk on your knees for a hundred miles through the desert, repenting." The gift of life is to be celebrated, not demeaned.

I've tried that. The repenting, that is. Not in the extreme forms we know exist, but trying to earn God's attention, God's blessing, God's love. We know it still happens. And, it will be interesting to see if repentance will be on the ascendancy in the days to come, once again requiring our Universalist answer of love.

"You only have to let the soft animal of your body love what it loves." Sometimes I wonder what I might have thought if my Scottish Baptist Preacher, Pastor Bellshaw, had said those words just once in my little church back home. He probably wouldn't have had his job for long. And it would have been very confusing to my young mind, going against everything else I was being taught at church.

Now, if your mind just jumped to the limits of acting on sexual impulses, you have proven that you are a child of the Puritans. Because if we believe that our humanity is a wildness that must be tamed, and our loving is a force that must be constrained, then it is pretty hard to figure out who we are and what it is we truly love. "You only have to let the soft animal of your body love what it loves."

I have been living with this poem for about a year now. The people in our "Living by Heart" class can witness to my stumbling reciting of the part of the poem I know each month as we have met. But what I haven't said yet to them is that the practice of "Letting the soft animal of your body love what it loves" was, for me, a surprise because I was so busy being careful of it. I say this because I know I'm not the only one. When I tried to be consciously aware of what I loved, I found it hard.

I think, sometimes, in our fear of over-loving one another, we can lose track of love itself—the love that flows from the center of our beings and is not only our own, but comes from the deepest source of life itself. We have become so preoccupied with sex as a culture, as a people, that love has become something to be constrained, restrained, bounded—and our hearts have become starved for the love that is all around us. The love that is the *gift* of our humanity, not the *curse* of it.

It is here that Mary Oliver makes such an interesting turn in her poem. "Tell me about despair, yours, and I will tell you mine." This being good doesn't give us much room to tell one another about our despair. This is, of course, why we try so hard to be good. For if we are afraid that lifting the boundaries on our goodness will create chaos—if not in the society, at least in our lives—opening ourselves to our own and each others' despair threatens to melt us into blobs of depression and anxiety.

When in reality, telling one another about our despair—if we can resist the temptation to say "there's a lesson for us in this" or "you will be a better person because of this" or any other version of self-protection—can open us to love.

Because, "meanwhile the world goes on". It does not stop to wait for us to be better, get better, do better, repent . . . "Meanwhile the sun and the clear pebbles of the rain are moving across the landscapes . . . Meanwhile the wild geese are heading home again."

I can imagine all those people trying to be good, looking up. The ones who are, perhaps for the first time in their lives, letting themselves notice love all around them—looking up. All of us about our daily business, going here and there, looking up, and wondering about that internal mechanism that says to the geese, "Go home." And so they leave their place, and head out in a "V" formation that allows them to travel much farther than they could alone. And, we're told, they rotate the duty of flying at the point so no one goose becomes overtired.

"The geese are out by the river," my mother told me a couple of weeks ago. That would be the Stanislaus River in the Central Valley of California. There is a large marshland not far from my mother's ranch and she drives out there to watch the geese this time of year. They will stay there a few weeks before venturing further north.

She knows about despair, though she doesn't talk about it much. She knows about loneliness, too, and she does mention that. At 94 her husband (my father), her sister, her friends, all have died. And she knows more than I do about the wild geese. We sometimes drive out and watch the geese together, when I am there.

Mary Oliver says, "Whoever you are, no matter how lonely, the world offers itself to your imagination." Now *here's* some important theology. Not a theology of goodness. Not a theology of sin and repentance. Not even a theology of redemption. Oliver does not suggest we can talk each other out of our loneliness or despair. Hers is a theology of the imagination.

If you think that is a flimsy excuse for a theology, spend some time watching wild geese, harsh and exciting, flying overhead. Calling out to us? Probably not. To one another? Maybe. But calling out, nonetheless. Drawing our vision upward, beyond ourselves. And, Mary Oliver says, "announcing our place in the family of things."

A long time ago, I realized that what was commonly known as a mid-life crisis was actually a failure of the imagination. This is when life, as we know it, falls away for one reason or another—be it death, divorce, loss of faith in what we had come to cherish, or any number of ways that things fall apart. Then, it is up to us to re-imagine ourselves, re-imagine our world. But not until I read this poem and found myself deep in mid-life did I realize that what we really need to do is re-imagine "our place in the family of things."

In the 13th Century, Rumi said, "Out beyond ideas of right doing and wrong doing—there is a field—I'll meet you there."[2] Mary Oliver is saying, "Let's all meet out there in that field." The field beyond right doing and wrong doing, where we can once again find our place in the family of things.

What *is* all this, but finding one's place in the family of things? And he feels "for a time the day-blind stars waiting with their light . . . For a time I rest in the grace of the world, and am free." That is one of the most succinct statements of our very human, very grounded theology: "I rest in the grace of the world, and am free."

So now, if you must . . . you can worry again (I hope not so much) about being good. I know I will. And you can keep your despair to yourself. And you can worry about love and proper boundaries and appropriateness. And you can forget to listen to your heart when it tells you that love is all around, all the time, and you need only to let the soft animal of your body love what it loves. And, if you must, you can miss the geese when they fly by, head down in work and worry.

But I hope sometime, in the next week or so, you will listen to the call to your imagination. The one that offers itself like the wild geese, over and over, announcing your place in the family of things. The place that is connected in freedom and love to all that is. The place that allows you to rest in the grace of the world and be free.

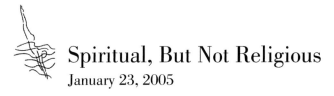

Spiritual, But Not Religious
January 23, 2005

*This sermon describes the painting on the cover of this book. It is
perhaps the first time I spoke directly about the depth found within a
religion, within the rituals, stories, and very real people who come to
church, serve their community and continue traditions handed to them
by their religious ancestors. LH*

From *With Open Hands*
By Henri Nouwen

To be calm and quiet by yourself is not the same as sleeping. In fact, it means being fully awake and following with close attention every move going on inside you. It requires the discipline to recognize the urge to get up and go again as a temptation to look elsewhere for what is close at hand. It offers the freedom to stroll in your inner yard and rake up the leaves and clear the paths so you can easily find the way to your heart . . . We recapture our own life afresh, from within. Along with the new knowledge of our 'inner space' where feelings of love and hate, tenderness and pain, forgiveness and greed are separated, strengthened, or reformed, there emerges the mastery of the gentle hand. This is the hand of the gardener who carefully makes space for a new plant to grow.[1]

From *The Living Pulpit*
By Maren Tirabassi

It has taken me longer in my ministry to recognize the Holy Prosaic as well as the Holy Mysterious. One strategy I have used in many years of leading retreats for lay people, seminarians, and clergy associations has always resulted in incredible gifts of insight for me. I invite people to bring something "holy" from their churches. These are a few of my favorite fragments of holiness—the key to the ladies' parlor, chalk from a Sunday School blackboard, a pot from the potluck, a photo of youth group members serving supper to homeless folk, the littlest angel costume from the Christmas pageant, shards of broken glass from "that weird worship" the seminarian did with the scripture about "Who-throws-the-first-stone a jar of grape jelly for a shut-in made of leftover Eucharist, the organist's slippers, the mimeograph machine "we might have a use for someday," the gift-certificate for a massage given to the preacher the Monday after

Easter, mortgage ashes, or a bulb from an Easter lily that just won't die. These things are holy.[2]

Some of you have found our church through Beliefnet.com. You took the quiz on this website to see which faith your profile resembled, and found you were closest to Unitarian Universalist, or Secular Humanist, or Quaker, in some order of the three. Then, I've been told that some of you, not knowing what Unitarian Universalist meant, moved to the Unitarian Universalist website, then linked to our website, and . . . here you are. Almost every time we have a group of new members join, someone in the group has found us through Beliefnet.com.

It may interest some of you that Beliefnet.com now has a feature called "Soulmatch," a matching service to help you meet people online with your same values and characteristics. In the initial quiz—to introduce you to the service—you can check, among other things, what faith you would prefer your matches to have. The list starts with "Any", and after the second on the list, shows all the usual main religions of the world. It is the second one that caught my eye: "Spiritual, but Not Religious."

I know exactly what that means. I've heard many here use just that phrase to describe themselves. I expect that a large number of people check that box on Soulmatch, so your chances would be good to meet someone if you also checked it. I also guess that if those people who checked "Spiritual, but Not Religious" met, fell in love and decided to marry, they would have a high probability of having their wedding at a Unitarian Universalist church. Because many would imagine that we are also "Spiritual, but Not Religious."

Once, in my first meeting with a couple planning their wedding, a young man told me that they came to this church for their wedding because they didn't like organized religion. I chose not to explain to him that we, in fact, *are* an organized religion, even knowing that John Buehrens—who preceded me as Senior Minister of this church—is known to have said, "You don't have to worry about organized religion around here. We're not that organized."

I didn't go into details because I knew what he meant. I know what people mean when they say they're spiritual but not religious. They mean they choose not to affiliate with any religious body of beliefs, doctrines, rituals and activities, perhaps because they have found them oppressive, or perhaps because they've never experienced them. There are, now, many people known in church-lingo as "the unchurched." They might say they are spiritual but not religious because they are the *adult children* of people who left organized religion long ago, never exposing them to any organized religion—making them wary of all of them.

People who say they are "spiritual, but not religious" mean that they have found meaning and purpose and even a set of beliefs about life and its mysteries outside Catholic, Jewish, Protestant Christian, or the "other" faiths on the Soulmatch list. They have found them in the writings of people like Jack

Kornfield, or Ram Dass, or Thich Nhat Hanh. Interestingly, each of these writers speaks out of a religious tradition, but don't directly represent that religion. They speak more to people outside religion altogether than to those who are churched. Or, these seekers may have found their spiritual path in the midst of poets like Rilke, Rumi, or Rabindranath Tagore, who speak eloquently of the life of the spirit and give guidance about how to live that life. Some have become spiritual but not religious because they have found more truth in nature than in church.

Whatever the source of their spiritual awakening, I know it can be transformative, sustaining, deeply meaningful and purposeful. It is, as we heard in the reading earlier, the call to go within. It is the call to pay attention to what is close at hand. It is the call to notice the feelings we have in the moment, but to move beneath them, to a deeper response, a deeper connection than our usual reactions and responses in life. It is an invitation to dip into the *underground river* (according to Ira Progoff),[3] or the *singing river* (according to Harry Scholefield),[4] the call to greet life *with open hands* (as Henry Nouwen suggested). Telling us to move into the *inner space* of our lives.

I have a postcard I keep on my desk. I received it in 1995 from Douglas Wilson, a colleague I barely know who had heard me preach, and said the picture on the postcard reminded him of my sermon. On the postcard is a reproduction of a painting by a contemporary Italian painter, Wainer Vaccari. The painting is titled "Deep Down." In very clear imagery, a man is poised on his toes at the top of a cliff, like a diver on a high diving board. Arms and hands pointed straight down, body bent as if he is already beginning the fall. His head is turned to the side away from us. He is looking at a figure floating above him. The figure has one outstretched arm pointing straight down. The horizon of the sea off in the distance, about even with the diver, is pale blue. But the sea into which he is about to dive is deep and dark. We know he's diving anyway.

I keep that postcard on my desk in a plastic envelope to protect it, because it reminds me—when I am tempted to scoot along the surface of things—that my call is to the depths. Not to the darkness *per se*—though sometimes that's what I find—but to the depths of life's purpose and meaning. To dive in. To dive off. To dive. The man's head is turned as if to say, "Are you sure?" And the angel's posture—no frilly wings in sight—says, "I'm sure."

I say this because it takes courage to live the spiritual life. It takes a willingness to face reality. To stop and face reality. It takes courage to take life on life's terms, and to dive deeply into its truths. It takes discipline to live a spiritual life. It takes silence and practice writing about fears and hopes and yearnings and thanks and regrets and joys. And being willing to start each day anew, as if it were your first.

But once in a while when someone tells me they're spiritual but not religious, I can sense a cop-out. They live in the world of shallow affirmations, and drippingly sweet words of inspiration. They live in the world of *imagined* joy, where tragedy never visits, and where love overcomes every difficulty. To be sure, our bookstores are chock full of books to sustain that vision. Today I want to honor the spiritual path that has depth, meaning, discipline, and a willingness to live without knowing what exactly is expected of us in the present moment—and living that moment as fully as we can anyway.

And I understand that religion has failed many people who have found their spiritual path on their own. I understand that religion has failed many who put their faith in belief systems and have been broken by them. I understand that religion has bored people until they couldn't stand it any more. And I understand that religion has excluded, restricted, and ruled over many people until they said "no more" and left.

So if you get anything from today, it is that I understand why people say, "I'm spiritual, but not religious." I get it. But, lest you find yourself embarrassed because you don't understand fully where you are, I want to add some thoughts about being religious.

One of the problems with being spiritual, but not religious—and it may be why some of you are here—is that it's hard to find a group to join. Some find a meditation group. Some who are spiritual, but not religious will have found their way into Group Therapy, or into a 12-Step group, and it will satisfy their need for companionship along the sometimes difficult road of life. For we will gather in groups—it seems to be part of human nature—to find others like us, to find others facing the same questions and challenges. To celebrate our joys together. We *will* find groups.

Now that it's on Soulmatch, and couples are encouraged to find each other, perhaps a larger "Spiritual but not Religious" movement will begin to emerge. Because eventually some of those couples will have children and will want to raise their children in a setting congruent with their world view. And then they may want to get together for spiritual practice. And then they may discover that others throughout time have done similar things, and *voila!* They're spiritual and religious at the same time.

Or they can come *here* for their religion. If you take anything else home today from this sermon, I need to say that coming here *is* a religious act. This is a religious place. We encourage you to be spiritual *and* religious here. But, you may say, this is a "dogma-free zone"—as one of our little www. UUDecide.com cards says. And doesn't dogma define religion? Sometimes. But more definitive is the history of grappling with theological questions. We have that. More definitive is a defined set of values. We have that. Even more definitive is the institution that is dedicated to a certain path, a certain set of activities—like teaching our children, and meeting here every Sunday to sing and pray and, for this brief time, order our lives together. And, probably *most* definitive is the extended past and future in which we honor those who have gone before and invest ourselves in the people and events that will follow us.

Someone said to me recently, "If you want your life to have meaning, invest in an institution." Invest your time and resources in the structures of society that have depth and meaning and purpose beyond your individual life.

On Friday, a friend of mine died. He was the husband of one of my best friends. They belong to the Unitarian Universalist Church in Bloomington, Indiana, where I was the minister for six years. Our friendship has continued over the 18 years since I was there.

My friend was 70. He was an ecologist who taught at Indiana University. Also, and more frequently than he liked, he gave expert testimony in cases around ecological issues. Usually about wetlands, his specialty. His life was invested in the preservation of wetlands, in the students who would carry the work forward, and in his Unitarian Universalist church. He sang in the choir—not always on key. He played the banjo in a string band. He first questioned and then agreed with the building of a sanctuary for that church. He questioned and then agreed with the hiring of three part-time ministers for that church in recent years. He was chair of the Grounds Committee in recent years, and spent untold hours at the church planting, trimming, mowing, and tending the grounds of the church. He mentored my son in the Coming of Age program. A better mentor I could not have found. When my son traveled to Bloomington to see his friends during his college days in Minnesota, he would stay with Dan and Melinda. He had a home there with them.

Dan did not claim to be spiritual or religious. He chided me frequently about my use of traditional religious language. He sided with Emerson and Thoreau about the power of nature to feed our souls. He found refreshment in 'catch and release' deep-sea fishing. In these last months of his life—far too brief a time as far as Dan's friends were concerned—in a specific shift of theological stance, he said that he found God in the community that surrounded and sustained him.

Last week the choir at their rehearsal called his home and sang one of their pieces to him through the phone. He couldn't speak anymore, but I'm told he smiled through the whole of the singing. The string band made regular visits to his home to the very end. Almost every Christmas card I received this year mentioned Dan and his illness. The church in Bloomington is in deep mourning today.

I tell you this personal story because it is my most recent experience with what it means to be religious. It is to be spiritual within the context of a living, breathing, sustaining, historically grounded institution with babies being born, old ones who are dying, and everything in between. It is to be spiritual within the context of potlucks and discussion groups, Sunday school classrooms, Christmas pageants and choir practice. It is to be spiritual and to take on a mortgage for expansion, and it is to be spiritual when it comes time to burn that mortgage.

To be spiritual *and* religious is to show up here each week. To bring your discouraged and sometimes battered spirit to this place to be lifted up, to be challenged, to be sustained here among all these others and to be blessed back into the world to continue your work—the investment of the time and resources of your life in things which matter.

To be spiritual *and* religious is to show up here each week, in this place where the two come together, where we search the inner space of our lives together. Where we, one more time, make space for hope to emerge, together. Where we are not alone in our grief. Not alone in our search. Where we are not alone.

So . . . all this is to say that the next time someone speaks to you about your faith, tell them your have found First Unitarian Church, where your spiritual life is nurtured, and where you have found a *religion* of inclusion, freedom, faith and hope for your life, for your family, for our future together. Tell them you are spiritual and religious, and that it has made all the difference.

More than Enough
April 24, 2005

That day the congregation repeated Dayenu as I told the highlights of our story as a church. There has always been more than enough for us as a congregation. It was a powerful moment in the sanctuary, when we all acknowledged it by saying Dayenu. I think it is one of the reasons it was picked as a favorite. LH

Psalm 104—Stephen Mitchell Translation (excerpts)

Unnamable God, you are fathomless;
    I praise you with endless awe.
You are wrapped in light like a cloak;
    you stretch out the sky like a curtain.
You make the clouds your chariot;
    you walk on the wings of the wind.
You use the winds as your messengers,
    thunder and lightning as your servants.
You look at the earth—it trembles;
    you touch the hills and they smoke.
You laid the earth's foundations
    so that they would never be destroyed.

You plant the trees that grow tall,
    pines, and cedars of Lebanon,
in which many birds build their nests,
    and the stork on the topmost branches.
The mountains are for the wild goats;
    the cliffs are a shelter for the rock squirrels.
You created the moon to count months;
    the sun knows when it must set.
You make darkness, it is night,
    the forest animals emerge.,
The young lions roar for their prey,
    seeking their food from God.

How infinite are your creatures, Unnamable One!
    With wisdom you made them all.
    The whole earth is filled with your riches . . .
I will sing to you at every moment;
    I will praise you with every breath.

How sweet it is to trust you;
    what joy to embrace your will.
May all selfishness disappear from me,
    and may you always shine from my heart.[1]

The Bible is full of stories about "more than enough." Problems happen. God provides. God rescues. God takes care. God watches over His people. He even knows when a sparrow falls to the ground. I saw a tiny lifeless sparrow last week on the side of a street where I was walking and I remembered that teaching. God knows, I thought. Or at least Life knows, if there is any consciousness in the life force that breathes us, until our last sigh.

The Bible is full of stories about "more than enough." Certainly the ritual celebration of Passover reminds us—even as it reminds our Jewish friends—that any one of the multiple gifts of life would be sufficient. But there was and is so much more . . . *Dayyenu.*

I have said this before, but it certainly felt true this week. Every time I pick a title for a sermon, I seem to have to live it (much more than I would choose) before I can preach it. And that was certainly true this week. In what ministers call "event convergence"—which is not a mystical term, it just means a lot of things happening at once—this week was full of great joys, startling needs, and a few surprises. Taken one-by-one, they would have found their regular place in my calendar.

The two weddings were planned. The three Memorial Services were not. The visit of my granddaughter—who brought her parents along last weekend—was planned. Some difficult turns regarding my son's job search were not. The joy of Scott and Kathy Baradell at their marriage was a delight. His brother's stroke the night following the wedding was not.

And, when I suddenly realized—in the midst of a phone call with a friend in Maine who started chemotherapy last week—that the wedding rehearsal at Perkins Chapel was at 6:00, not 7:00 as I had imagined, and it was exactly six o'clock and I was at my home, I had a profound sense of insufficiency.

I had to laugh at myself, driving to the chapel. God may be sufficient—that was to be the message today—but I was beginning to feel decidedly *insufficient.* It was one more time, it seemed, of having to live the question I was preaching, before I would preach it. Notice, I don't preach about death much!

I should say that when I got there—after making a somewhat panicked call to my assistant, Susan Schmidt, to meet me there with the wedding service, safely on my desk here at the church—the sister of the bride, who was a wedding planner, had the rehearsal well in hand. The organist was playing, the attendants were in their places, and the bride and her father were about to go down the aisle. They were glad to see me, but didn't seem disturbed that I was a half hour late.

I hasten to add that this is not my usual practice. It's just been one of those weeks. We all have them! And from what I hear, we have them fairly consistently. All our well-laid plans to keep our lives in balance, to be organized, not to over-commit—are overcome by life and its small and large surprises.

I seemed, this week, to be living the question of sufficiency right out to the edge of my own resources of time and energy. I couldn't help noticing, as the week progressed, that this question of sufficiency must be about something different than keeping the "convergence of events" at bay and fending off any further "commitment creep".

I remembered the verse in Isaiah I memorized as a child, "But they that wait upon the Lord shall renew their strength; they shall mount up with wings as eagles; they shall run, and not be weary; and they shall walk, and not faint." This is a wonderful poetic image of soaring with the wings of an eagle, of being free. In my childhood mind, I thought it meant that I would never be tired, or weary. Of course, as a child, I didn't know what waiting had to do with it, either.

The story of Passover is about freedom as well. But that freedom is about a people. It doesn't have anything to do with what one poet has called, "The colossal hoax of clocks and calendars."[2] Passover is a ritual story about the freedom of a people who had been enslaved. Like most, if not all, ritual stories of identity, it has its miracles, it has its moments of rescue: God brings plagues on the Egyptians until they're glad to get rid of the Israelites. Then they change their minds, chase them to the edge of the Red Sea, and the sea parts to let the Israelites through.

Some have said in recent days that this image may have come from an experience with a Tsunami. Perhaps so. But the miracle of the story is muddled. Not only did the Egyptians change their minds, but after the Israelites were truly free, they began to complain: "We'd rather be slaves in Egypt. At least then we had food and shelter. Now we don't know where our next meal is coming from and we're wandering in the desert." Moses had his hands full keeping them from going back.

What *is* this sufficiency, this more than enough, that is so much a part of the observance of Passover each year? First let me tell you what I think it is not. It is not a celebration of God's protection. I have a colleague who says, "If that's what being a Chosen People means, I'd rather not be chosen." These Chosen People are a confused, complaining, idol-building, wandering bunch. In what may be the first story about what freedom means, they prefer slavery over freedom. It's *not* a celebration of God's protection. Freedom is risky, confusing, and frightening.

It's also not a story about lessons learned. I hear this often, even here, that some difficulty or another has been a lesson given us by life to refine our character. There are lessons to be learned in life, to be sure. But the Passover story is not about that. If it is, the Israelites aren't very good examples, as they learn over and over—and over—the lesson of trust. (And it's unclear whether they ever really learn it, even when they see the Promised Land.) No, I don't think it's about lessons learned.

And it's not even about "slowing down." This is more obvious. The Israelites had to leave Egypt in haste. "Run for their lives" might be a way to say it. They had to leave beloved possessions behind. They didn't have time to make bread for the journey, in the usual way—no time to let it rise. They had to eat unleavened bread, one reason that, even today during Passover Jews remove leavening from their homes and eat Matzoth (unleavened bread). There was no time. So, it's not even about 'taking time' to reflect, or leaving spaces in our schedules. We run for our lives in a different way, but we can understand when the story says, the Israelites left Egypt in haste.

So, if it's not about God's special protection and blessing of us (Even if you don't believe in God, I'm willing to bet at least some of you feel you're special or unique. It's not about that) . . . .

If it's not about lessons to learn (Lord knows we have lots to learn. But what if the events of our lives—even events as large in ritual life as the passage of the Israelites out of slavery—aren't especially planned to teach us things?) . . .

If it's not about 'slowing down,' taking time, becoming more reflective (although, let me be the first to say that's a good idea, even if it's not what this ritual story is about) . . .

Then, what *is* it? What truth is there for us? (Why do I have to get to the end of my rope, as it were, to preach this sermon?)

I think the answer lies, first, in recognizing that it is a ritual story of a whole people, not individuals. There are individuals mentioned along the way. We know a lot about the Pharaoh, Moses and Aaron. But the story is not about them. So reading it as a story to tell us how to live as individuals misses the point.

It is a story about a people.

Any difficulty I might have with "event convergence" I may have to figure out, but *Dayyenu* doesn't have anything to do with my daily schedule. We are so steeped in the idea of individualism; we can easily miss the reality that a ritual story such as Passover is about a people. We, who are so quick to interpret events, even in our own time, as they relate to our individual lives, forget that we are a people.

And even those of us here today—who come with a yearning perhaps for a little wisdom, a little comfort, some good music, to see our friends, to meet some like-minded people—can miss what is happening here. Each Sunday, the boundaries might change a bit as we redefine who we are. The faces sitting next to you might change, as people come or don't come to this or that service. But over the course of time, as Passover reminds us, we—who celebrate a certain approach to life, who meet here in a cycle of rituals through the year, who week after week present ourselves here—are also a people. And we, too, like the Israelites, like the Jews of today, celebrate freedom.

Oh, I have my rights. And you have yours. And I am profoundly grateful for them. I have my obligations and you have yours, and I try to be sensitive to those, as well. But *dayyenu*—the ritual observance of sufficiency—has to do with the whole, with all of us, together.

So, in case you don't know the story—here's a very brief telling:

When there was no voice for Liberal Christianity in Dallas, 32 people gathered in 1899 to form this church . . . *Dayyenu.*

And the church grew, and freedom of thought and belief was found there . . . *Dayyenu.*

During the depression, the church doors closed, and the people wandered in the desert, even as the Women's Alliance continued to meet . . . *Dayyenu.*

The church re-opened its doors, and became a haven for those lost without a chart and a compass for their spiritual lives . . . *Dayyenu.*

The people moved from their place of meeting, to land of their own . . . *Dayyenu.*

They built a home for religious freedom; three times they built—for fellowship, for children's religious education, for sanctuary . . . *Dayyenu.*

And the people became known across their land, for courage in the face of trials, for liberty in the face of spiritual and political bondage, for strength in the face of fear and suspicion . . . *Dayyenu.*

And liberty came and dwelt among them—and many women claimed new power because of it . . . *Dayyenu.*

And men who were gay and women who were lesbians found new life in this place . . . *Dayyenu.*

And those who grieved were comforted, and those who made public and life-long promises to one another were celebrated, and the babies were brought to the sanctuary to be blessed and children were nurtured . . . *Dayyenu.*

And freedom took root, and held them firmly in the days of trials, so that they would not be shaken . . . *Dayyenu.*

And for all this they praised God, whom they knew by many names—and as mystery unnamable . . . *Dayyenu.*

The more than sufficiency of the God of the Israelites is a celebration of a rather rag-tag group of people incredibly chosen by God to fulfill certain purposes, not the least of which was to create a story of freedom from slavery. Ours is no less a story of significance. It's just that in our frenetic everyday lives, we can mistake that celebration of sufficiency for a definition of how much we have as individuals of time, of purpose and even of spiritual depth.

But the story of our freedom is more than individual. It is a story of our tribe, our people, here in Dallas for more than 100 years. Admittedly that's not 4,000 years. But, with freedom's power, we may be here that long. Meanwhile, for over 100 years here in Dallas we have stood for something: the power of freedom, to open the mind and heart, to break the bonds of literalism and oppression, to create a place where people can find their way out of the desert, out of the wilderness—where people can find their way home.

What we have been given is so much more than sufficient. It is more than we might expect. It is certainly more than we have claimed for our future. Freedom's gifts are bountiful. May we recognize that we have "more than enough." *Dayyenu.*

What If You Knew Then, What You Know Now
May 22, 2005

I'm never sure when I preach a sermon like this one, whether I am a voice of one, or the voice of many. Perhaps, I think, everyone else knew all this, and I was the only one who didn't. But just in case, I preached it, and it resonated with many people in the congregation. I really do wish someone had told me these things back when I was twenty-two. But in case there's someone else out there who needs to hear it, here it is! LH

For Everything a Season
Ecclesiastes 3

For everything there is a season,
and a time for every matter under heaven:
A time to be born, and a time to die;
A time to plant, and a time to
pluck up what is planted;
A time to kill, and a time to heal;
A time to break down, and a time to build up;
A time to weep, ande a time to laugh;
A time to mourn, and a time to dance;
A time to throw away stones,
and a time to gather stones together;
A time to embrace, and a time to refrain from embracing.
A time to seek, and a time to lose;
A time to keep, and a time to throw away;
A time to tear, and a time to sew;
A time to keep silence, and a time to speak;
A time to love, and a time to hate;
A time for war,
And a time for peace.

An excerpt from *The Layers*
By Stanley Kunitz

In my darkest night,
when the moon was covered
and I roamed through wreckage,
a nimbus-clouded voice
directed me:
"Live in the layers,
not on the litter."

> Though I lack the art
> to decipher it,
> no doubt the next chapter
> in my book of transformations
> is already written.
> I am not done with my changes.[1]

Every once in awhile I ruminate on what kind of life I would have lived, had I known then (back when I was young) what I know now. I will say at the outset that, as far as questions go, this is not a good one. Rilke, as many of you may know, said that we should live the questions, and that perhaps someday we will discover we have lived into the answers. This isn't one of those questions that can be lived into, because it takes us backwards—it's the wrong direction for creative living. But even with that said—even when I know it's not a fruitful venture—I do this sort of ruminating. What was I thinking? I ask myself, when I made certain decisions, and didn't make others. The best I can come up with is that I was doing the best I could, given what I *did* know.

There was a time, back then, when I resolved to live without regret. It seemed to me that if one were to put one's mind to it, one could live a life without regret. You just had to stay alert, think clearly, act decisively, and be good! I can't say now that I regret much unless it was that very determination to be good, for it tripped me up more than the catalogue of imagined sins I feared.

Because many of us, no matter how many years we have lived, learn pretty quickly that being able to manage how things will come out is a nice idea, but it's not how life works. We do our best. We do what we can. Some of our best intentions have bad results. And some of our stupidest mis-steps turn out to be life changing in surprising and often very good ways.

Our intentions are important. I believe we have to be well-intended, no matter what, but I have to preach the truth. The truth is that our intentions, no matter how lofty and grand, have unintended consequences. Sometimes they're better than we imagined, sometimes worse, often a little of both.

So, I wish I'd known, back when I was, say, 22, that it would be impossible to get it right. I would tell that 22 year-old that there really isn't a "right" to get. That even though I was raised on a healthy dose of cowboys in white and black hats, in real life it wasn't so easy to tell the good from the bad-that it was all mixed together, and probably the more sure I was about who was wearing which hat, the less likely I would be to see my way. It feels dangerous to say—even now, these many years later—that there isn't a clear right and wrong about things because on the surface there is right and wrong. There *are* qualities of living which distinguish the moral from the immoral, the honest from the dishonest, the true from the false, and I am grateful for the training that helped me know what they are. But then—and this is the dangerous part—at some point, and it's usually quite a jolt when it happens, we realize that knowing the rules isn't enough. That knowing right from wrong isn't enough. That there's a life to be lived on terms different from what we were taught. (Or at least I can say, "On terms different from what *I* was taught.")

I envy our young people, raised to know that ambiguity is part of life, and—though they may not fully perceive what it will mean in their lives—they will not have to see life through a completely different lens from the lens of their childhood, as some of us have had to do. I've spoken here before about my own difficulty making that shift, and today I will admit that I envy our own young people's ability to grasp the complexity of life, and claim the values of good character. They will not be spared the hard discoveries along the way. But at least they won't have to start over, when they reach adulthood.

That said, I think all of us have been surprised by the multiple lives we have lived—even the most well settled and secure of us. Somehow, back then, there was the belief that you prepared yourself for adulthood and then lived it. Maybe everybody but me knew that they would live many lives, "Some of them our own" as Stanley Kunitz said in his poem. At the age of 95, he was saying "I'm not done with my changes." He was still writing poetry last year, at 99. As far as I know, he is still not done with his changes at 100. (Perhaps you have heard of his death, but I have not).

This week I had an interesting conversation with a colleague. Her Father had died. Her Mother wanted her to come home. Her church was not an easy one; it was hard to have a personal life in the small town where she lived, and the year had been especially difficult. At one point last fall, she was seriously considering quitting the ministry and going home. When I talked with her this week, her first words were, "Well, I decided to stay." She had begun to see some opportunities both where she was, and with a move. Her Mom had a puppy which had become a companion and was beginning to create her own new life. She said—and I believe these are perhaps the most important words one could say—"I've decided this is my life, and I might as well live it."

I knew that, in a way, back then. Life wasn't just going to happen to me. I had to forge, to form, to hammer it out, no matter what the circumstances. I may have been a little fierce about it back then. I came from a family of hard workers, and I tended to approach all the situations of my life with the belief that if you worked hard enough it could be overcome. I wish I had known that approach, while it has its rewards, isn't always the best one. That tenacity will get you through, but it doesn't always build a life that is yours.

I remember specifically when I realized that I wasn't living my parent's lives. My Father was having open heart surgery, and I realized that he would die—if not then, some other day. And I'd better have my own life, or I would die with him. It propelled me, startlingly, into the ministry.

I wish I'd known before then, that I would "walk through many lives, some of them my own." And that once I had realized what my own life could look like, I would get better at making sure the one I was living at any point in time, at least resembled my own. That it would be a continual process of claiming and reclaiming my life, its form in any given moment shaped by the needs of the time.

I wish I'd known I'd be making myself "a tribe out of my true affections." Stanley Kunitz describes the scattered tribe, in his 90's. I know what he means. But I wish I'd known that deep friendships and true affections wouldn't be limited to a small circle in one place. Forty years ago, I thought they would be.

For some they are. I went back to my High School reunion a few years ago, and ran into an old boyfriend. He lived two blocks from the home he had grown up in. His wife was from there. Their grown children lived near. He went to the same church. I was surprised that I was surprised. But even he had lived many lives, some of them his own. His tribe looked as if it were the same, but I'm guessing he too could say "he had made himself a tribe out of his true affections", even if perhaps not as scattered as some.

I wish I'd known back then that I wouldn't have to do it alone. Those friends, even as inadequate as I was for the journey, would be companions along the way, and become part of my tribe.

I wish I'd known that my first big loss was not going to be my last. How devastated I was back then. And I had to be. It was the first big transition from one life to another. From one life only partially my own, to another, eventually claimed-that was more fully mine.

I wish I'd known becoming ourselves comes in fits and starts, and never ends.

I wish I'd known that grief (Kunitz calls it "the slow fire trailing from the abandoned campsites") that grief would carve a place in my soul, but that I would live to tell the story. (At the time I wasn't sure.) And those other lives would come to tear away the false shell, and would teach me about my true affections.

And finally, I wish I had known to "Live in the layers, Not on the litter", a phrase Stanley Kunitz says just came to him. It is so easy to go back over losses, to rewrite the history in our minds, to ruminate, to cogitate, to imagine that if we get to the core of that difficulty we will be able to handle the ones we are living now. And while there is some truth to having an "examined life" there is more truth in the advice to live in the layers, not on the litter.

I once had a friend, a dear friend I had known a long time. In the middle of my rumination with her over something that had happened when we were in our thirties, she said, simply, "You were complicit." She'd heard the story before; she had known me when it happened. She'd probably listened to it one too many times. But her words stopped me in my tracks. I *had* been complicit.

At the time, that may have been the best I could do. But I had been complicit. And so, I realized I had to move on. To let go of that thin thread back into a life that certainly no longer was mine, if it ever had been.

There is a principle of being that we must cling to, in the midst of all the smoldering fires of past lives, in the midst of lives lived only partially. There is a principle of being we must cling to. I think I did know that, back then, perhaps always. Though I couldn't describe it well, I knew what it is. And, through all the changes, I have at least moved toward it. I'm glad I knew that.

We, none of us, are who we were. That is not a cause, I now know, for regret. Even the skeptic and realist writer of the ancient Ecclesiastes knew there were times for various lives, various tasks. Knowing this can make all the difference. Living it gives us hope. I wish I'd known it then. I do know it now. I hope, with Stanley Kunitz, that I can say, at 100 years, "I am not done with my changes." That's living without regret.

America's Real Religion
September 25, 2005

In our battle to keep our country from becoming a theocracy, this is a plea not to revert to secularism. There is a religious language 'of the public square' that calls us to la virtue that is not sectarian. We will have to enlarge our view of that language in the ever-increasing pluralism within which we live. But it is a challenge worth living. LH

From <u>America's Real Religion</u>
By A. Powell Davies

It is significant to recall that as President, Washington confirmed the constitutional principle that the government of the United States is not founded upon any *one* religion. In the Treaty with Tripoli, which he initiated (it was proclaimed later by President John Adams and finally ratified under Jefferson's administration) this is completely explicit. "The government of the United States," the Treaty says, "is not in any sense founded upon the Christian Religion." What this means is that the government of the United States is no more founded upon the Christian religion than upon the Jewish religion, or any other religion. It is founded upon freedom of religion.

But does all this signify that Washington himself had no religious faith? Was he—as his enemies insisted—an infidel? The word *infidel* means *without religious faith*. The only religious faith, however, that Washington was *without* was the faith of the creeds; the faith of traditional religious institutions.

That he believed—and deeply—in the higher religion that rejected the superstitions based on fear but reinforced the spiritual nature and moral capacity of man is attested by his adherence to American foundational principles. How else could he have thought that man was fit for liberty, or capable of building and maintaining a just society? [1]

The title of this sermon comes from a little book of sermons published in 1949 by A. Powell Davies, Minister of All Souls Church in Washington, D.C. from 1944 until his death in 1957. Davies was a Methodist minister who came to a Methodist Church in Portland, Maine in 1928. There he met Reverend Vincent Silliman, the minister of Portland's First Unitarian Church, and their deep friendship led him to an interest in our faith. Davies then moved to Summit, New Jersey, where he was minister of a non-denominational church that he moved into the American Unitarian Association. Eventually he was called to All Souls Unitarian Church in Washington, D.C., where he spent 13 significant years, serving his church, starting new churches—which to this day ring the city of Washington—giving radio speeches, writing magazine articles, books, and addresses which gave him a nationwide audience as a progressive thinker. When he suddenly died in 1957, the *Washington Post* said, "He was, among all the members of his calling, the most resolute and indomitable champion of righteousness as he saw it and of the brotherhood of man (sic). All men, indeed—all men who believe in human dignity and brotherhood—are the poorer for the passing of this courageous, fiery, and yet gentle spirit."[2]

Davies' most significant contribution to our movement was *America's Real Religion.* In it he was able to finesse the often treacherous waters of church and state, politics and religion, and give, for that time, one of the first cogent explanations of a faith that permeated our democracy but did not turn it into a theocracy. A faith that could promote the values of democracy but did not turn to any one religion as its primary source.

Some of you will find you disagree with Reverend Davies. I ask you to hold your concerns because, after I tell you what he fervently believed, I want to add some words about where we are now. In his book, Davies described the various beliefs of the "Founding Fathers". Let me say at the outset that we have come a long way in understanding the contributions of the "Founding Mothers", and they were substantial. But Davies—as progressive and clear as he was about the uses of language—was as limited by his time as we are now in ways we can't even imagine. Thus, he did not use gender inclusive language: Davies talked about the Men who founded our country. All the same, it was people like Davies—who called for inclusiveness at every level of thinking—who brought us to the time of possibility for men and women to be included equally.

What I hope to do is resolve some of the confusion we have about religious language in the public square, or at least about how it was conceived back then. Davies believed that fear was a great motivator in both religion and politics. He said, "Just as man enslaved his mind to superstition because he was afraid of the world about him, so he subjected his person to tyranny because he feared his fellow-men."[3] It hasn't been hard these last few weeks to see how such a fear takes hold. The powers of nature, the threat of lawlessness, the breakdown of security, can easily cause people to turn to superstition, or to the belief that events have come about like the biblical story of Noah, as a way God has of cleansing the world of sinners and 'starting over.'

Sometime after Hurricane Katrina, a minister said the storm was God's way of destroying the sinful city of New Orleans. Another minister reminded him publicly that many of his Christian brothers had lost their churches in that flood. This struggle has gone on as far back as we can remember. We try to find meaning in events (especially cataclysmic ones) and have plenty of scripture and doctrine to back us up. Great fears have given rise to dogmatic and judgmental religion. They also have given rise to tyranny.

Time will tell if the fallout from Hurricanes Katrina and Rita will include a rise in tyrannical government. At this point I'm not sure, since the belief that Government will take care of things has been so shaken. But we will see. The recognition that we are so significantly unprepared for an evacuation of any kind is sobering enough. Will that realization bring fear and submission or a new boldness, when it comes to choosing our leaders? We don't know yet.

But this certainly illustrates what fear could do in Davies' time, a time rife with anti-communism and the tyrannical blacklisting of people who were thought to be communists. Davies believed that Government and Religion had arisen over the centuries as a stay against fear, giving rise to tyranny and submission. His little book was a call to the higher religion upon which our country was founded.

Hindsight is wonderful. Knowing that Jefferson had slaves makes us wonder about his right to say that all men should be free. There were many discontinuities in what the Founding Fathers said and did. There always are. I imagine that for those who are truly leaders it is often impossible to live up to their vision of what might be. I imagine most of them know it, even as they speak of possibilities.

And so it was with Washington, Jefferson, John Adams, and Benjamin Rush—and all the others who struggled to forge this nation that would be based on freedom. Davies says (instead of fear),

> "came yearning—the kindlier outreach of the mind and heart—that made men feel that in the mystery about them there was something that responded to their loneliness. Just as from fear came superstition and the mind's enslavement, so from yearning came reassurance and release. There was courage, there was hope. Something could fill the lonely heart with song . . . the ultimate realities might be unknown, perhaps unknowable; yet there were insights. Existence might be harsh and cruel; yet there was gentleness. Thus there began to be new uses for imagination: instead of the nightmare, the dream; instead of the superstitious ritual, the poem; instead of the sacrifice, the psalm. Life could be good and happy; there was that which sometimes made it so. It could be happier in the future than the past: surely it would be.
>
> . . . Meanwhile, from *yearning* also came the need for human societies to cling together. It was not fear alone that formed the social groups. There was a growing sense of brotherhood, the fellowship of those who share a common fate. And just as fear, through necessity *forced* social groupings to enlarge, yearning *invited* it. Fear said: the

tribe is not strong enough, it cannot endure its own defense. It must be merged with other tribes to make a larger unit. But yearning said, the tribe is not good enough, it bars the way to what the heart cries out for: nothing is good enough except the unrestricted brotherhood of man . . . something reached out. A widening communion grew . . . Out of it came tenderness and sympathy, and new perceptions grew: (love) became the love that conquered fear. Here was the better key to unlock mysteries, here was the path to nobler living, the freeing of the mind, the fullness of the heart, the true redemption of the spirit.

. . . From *fear* came superstition and tyranny, with its burden of subjection and slavery. But from *yearning* came courage and liberation . . . . The conquest of fear produced *freedom of the mind* and a *widening brotherhood*—which . . . is the spiritual base of democracy."[4]

Yesterday, at our "Marriage and Moral Values Conference", Charles McMullen, our Director of Adult Religious Education, helped us work through the moral values implicit in marriage that take us out of a discussion of the issue of same gender or opposite gender rights, and into the deep values that are supported by marriage. That discussion can lead us to the obvious conclusion that, if the state of marriage holds these values for couples and for the larger society, it is then important that these values be upheld on behalf of all people. I will be saying more about this before the Constitutional Amendment defining marriage as the union of one man and one women will be voted on in November—an Amendment that has arisen out of fear.

But, today I want to focus on the spiritual base of democracy. Because, as you have heard me say if you have attended a Roots class, our country was founded on the three-legged stool of law, education, and virtue. Notice it was not founded on law, education, and *Christianity*. Not even law, education, and the Judeo-Christian tradition, as some call it.

The Founders believed that the churches, temples, and synagogues would, in their own way, provide the virtue necessary for the survival of the democracy. They also believed that all the churches would become 'non-creedal' (which didn't happen). Thomas Jefferson is reported as having said, "All young men by the next generation will become Unitarian" (which also didn't happen).

They came from many different religious traditions, but by the time they were forging a Constitution and the Law of the Land, however fragile it was, they pretty much had a sense this couldn't be a government based on power (tyranny) or guided by the leaders' interpretation of God's will (a theocracy). It had to be based on freedom *from* tyranny (they wouldn't have a king, no matter how benevolent) and freedom *from* religious hierarchy (they wouldn't serve a priest or pope, or any other spokesperson for God, no matter how wise).

But here's what I want you to know about those Founders: they believed that freedom would open us up to a new spirituality, call us to a higher level of morality. It would depend on an educated people, laws which counterbalanced the always-present lust for power, and churches that reminded people of the need of *la virtu*, the virtue necessary if a democracy was to survive. The leaders understood that people had their individual churches, but no one church would be the religion of the land. They also understood—and this is why I'm preaching this sermon today—that there could be a national humility that was best couched in appeals to God (not Jesus). That is why from the very beginning, prayers were said before every meeting of Congress. It was understood, even back then, that the prayers were not to be sectarian, but to a more general God, for a more general blessing upon our land.

For the Founders, the Ten Commandments were not a hammer down the throat of a secular culture, as they seem to have become, but rather a general statement of ethics. Jesus, if he was mentioned, was not the Jesus of creeds and doctrines, but a teacher of a high level of moral accountability to the poor, the weak, to those who are not free. It is this "real religion" of our democracy—sometimes called the American Democratic Faith, the faith that was the substantive grounding of our nation—that called us, decade after decade, to liberate, liberate, and continue to liberate, in the name of the survival of our democracy. To free *all* people from the bondages of creed and doctrine, unfair laws, and poor educational systems.

So, where are we today in the fulfillment of this very idealistic and startling formula that was set out by the founders of our country? First, we find what Unitarian Universalist Minister Forrest Church has called "The Failure of Our First Principle". It is how keenly aware we are, not only that we have fallen short of those lofty ideals, that these very men couldn't see what their principles meant in their own lives. Jefferson is one of the most public examples of that failure. Just as he was writing about freedom for all men (and we'll cut him a little slack—not much—on the issue of women), we can't fathom how he could then go home to his slaves, to say nothing of the children he fathered through his slave, Sally Hemings.

I do not condone this. I think a lot of problems in our country would have been easily solved if they had fully embodied, in our constitution and other founding documents, what they thought was the ideal. The truth is, they wrote and carved out a country that wasn't then and isn't now living up to the ideal they envisioned. We've had to climb a long hard road, not very pretty at that, to get to the freedoms we have today. They wrote ahead of what they lived.

But we who have legitimate concerns about the separation of church and state in this time when a theocracy seems to be looming behind the rhetoric of a lot of politicians, need to know that in their formula for democracy, radical though it was, was the belief that people (educated and called to virtue under laws that were fair) could uphold a government by the people, and for the people.

Now we know that the word "God" is not a generic term for all religion. Now we know that the Ten Commandments are not the be all and end all of ethical statements. Now we know that Jesus, even as just a moral teacher, is not the only teacher in the world. We have been thrust into a pluralistic world that our Founding Fathers had intimations of, but certainly not the understanding that we now have.

We must re-examine our language for the public square. But I preach this sermon not as a history lesson, but as a call to understand why religious language and symbols appeared in our public square *at all*. It was because we need to have a higher calling as a nation than government or even education can give us. They believed religion—especially the higher values of religion and the virtue it inspires in people—would help us in times of fear and in times when we would be tempted to leave democracy to others to maintain.

This leaves us with a difficult but important task: standing against the incursions of doctrinaire sectarianism in the public square. And at the same time, not being caught up in countering sectarianism with secularism, which takes the conversation away from virtue rather than toward it.

Our Unitarian ancestors believed in 'salvation by Character.' They believed that the highest manifestation of religion was in the ways it helped people live virtuous lives. It was in the values it promoted, crucial to our survival. Now we're trying to learn again how to speak to public issues in the language of values. The best place to learn this is here, at church. Not that we will not have our own little take on how things should be done, but because the language of inclusion, the language of hope, the language of humility, is badly needed. And we are the ones who have been the bearers of this tradition since the beginning.

This is not a time to be timid. America's Real Religion—if it is not to be consumerism, imperialism, or a valueless secularism—needs to remind people of their higher selves, the country of its nobler purposes, and our faith of its unique position in history to move us into a new day.

Marriage and Moral Values
October 23, 2005

One of the most wonderful weddings in our church was between a beloved Youth Leader and his partner. The youth in our church served as ushers. At the reception following, the women from the Women's Alliance danced with the men from the Lesbian and Gay group. Adults danced with children. Women with women. Men with men. It was a grand church-wide celebration. It was also a revolutionary event, right in the heart of Dallas. The couple eventually moved to Vermont, a state where they could enjoy legal rights. LH

From a selection by Theodore Parker, Unitarian Abolitionist Minister, who lived from 1810-1860.

It takes years to marry completely two hearts, even of the most loving and well-assorted. A happy wedlock is a long falling in love. Young persons think love belongs only to the brown-haired and crimson-cheeked. So it does for its beginning. But the golden marriage is a part of love which the Bridal day knows nothing of.

A perfect and complete marriage, where wedlock is everything you could ask and the ideal of marriage becomes actual, is not common, perhaps as rare as perfect personal beauty.

(We) are married fractionally, now a small fraction, then a large fraction. Very few are married totally, and they only after some forty or fifty years of gradual approach and experiment.

Such a large and sweet fruit is a complete marriage that it needs a long summer to ripen in, and then a long winter to mellow and season it. But a real, happy marriage of love and judgment . . . is one of the things so very handsome that if the sun were, as the Greek poets fabled, a God, he might stop the world and hold it still now and then in order to look all day long on some example thereof, and feast his eyes on (it.)[1]

Excerpts from I Corinthians 13

Love is patient; love is kind; love is not envious or boastful or arrogant or rude. It does not insist on its own way; it is not irritable or resentful, it does not rejoice in wrong doing, but rejoices in the truth. It bears all things, believes all things, hopes all things, endures all things . . .

When I was a child, I spoke like a child, I thought like a child, I reasoned like a child. When I became an adult, I put an end to childish ways. Now, we see in a mirror, in a riddle. Then we will see face to face. Now I know in part. Then I will know fully.

165

> Now faith, hope, and love abide, these three, and the greatest
> of these is love.

In 1981, when I was a new minister at the Unitarian Universalist Church of Bloomington, Indiana, home of Indiana University, I was approached by two women who wanted to have a Service of Union at the University Chapel. They had been told that they could have such a service if it was conducted by an Ordained Minister. Since I was the only Ordained Minister in the town who, at the time, could freely conduct such services, they called me.

My thinking was pretty simple then. Commitments and intentions to love, honor and cherish one another were good. I saw such commitments as the building blocks of our larger society. A ritual in which people made promises to one another, witnessed by friends and family, was good. I agreed to conduct the service. The woman who was the curator at the University Chapel did not seem to register any surprise when two women showed up for the rehearsal. My memory is that it was a lovely and joyous day.

One thing I wish I had done from the beginning of my ministry is to keep track of couples I have married. But, while I registered these women's names and the date of their service in my *Wedding Book*, I don't know what happened to them.

I was as naive as they were. Or perhaps more so, since I had not experienced what it took to get them to my office, in my church, with the intentions to commit their lives to one another. Oh, I had been married and divorced, myself. But I had no idea of the special circumstances involved in same-gender marriages.

I remember Thandeka's wonderful book, *Learning to be White*, in which she talks about what it takes for people of color to assimilate into a white culture. I did not know what it took for same gender couples to assimilate into a heterosexual world.

I didn't know how much a profession of fidelity before God and witnesses might satisfy certain needs, but would not make one iota of difference if they eventually divorced. If they did divorce, they would have no legitimate position to support their claims. I did not know that, however sacred their vows, they would not have legal rights to property if one of them died. And they would not be considered 'next of kin' in making all those important end-of-life decisions. I knew that in some ways (depending on where they lived), they might be 'accepted' as a committed couple but, back in 1981, I imagine that wasn't easy.

Some people were 'out' as a couple at church, but not at their jobs, 'out' with their siblings, but not with their parents. Every relationship, every new situation was a test of how safe it was to be open about their sexual identity and open about a same-gender partner.

I didn't know then, but I do know now, that it is important to have all the legal documents in place. Who has power of attorney? Who has the legal ability to make health care decisions, should it be necessary? Have they made wills?

Are their physician's directives in order? And on and on. Because, the irony of same gender unions is that they have made us all realize that the religious union and the legal union are two separate things. In same gender unions, there could be no legal assumptions.

I realized one day to my surprise that in many countries where there is no separation between Church and State, people are married down at the courthouse and then have a religious ceremony at the church. In weddings here in the United States—where we claim a serious separation of church and state—it is the one time I, as a minister, represent the state in a ceremony that is both a legal and religious event. Except of course, in the case of same gender unions.

In the early days of my ministry, same gender couples would come to me, wanting a service, but not wanting any of it to look like a wedding. If heterosexual couples would exchange rings, they would exchange bracelets. If heterosexual couples would repeat traditional vows, they would write their own. And so on. They were like the couples that would say they wanted an informal wedding, but hadn't given any thought to how they might enter and exit the church 'spontaneously.' Same gender couples often knew what they didn't want to have in their Service of Union. But weren't sure what they did want.

And then there were the couples that were homosexual, but in 'learning to be heterosexual' chose to marry people they loved who were of opposite gender. I once conducted a service in Bloomington for a lesbian woman and a gay man. They loved each other, and planned to have a life and family together. I tried to talk them out of it. But they were persuasive, and in the end, I was the minister of their church. So, I chose to stand on the side of love and commitment and officiated at their joyous wedding. All these years later (at least 20), after considerable pain and sadness, they are now married to same-gender partners. The wife in the couple is the mother of a teenager that she and her partner have raised.

It was a good idea, that wedding. But, like lots of good ideas that seem to be good at the time, it didn't work. It took a long time to come to the realization that their relationships had to grow out of who they were, not ideas of who they wanted to be.

I say all this because Texans will be asked to vote on Proposition 2 in the November eighth election. This proposition would amend our State Constitution to define marriage as the union of one man and one woman. It does not actually change the law. Our State Legislature endorsed the Defense of Marriage Act in 2003, so that any same gender marriages from our own or other states couldn't be recognized here. It also prohibits the State or any political subdivision in Texas from creating or recognizing any legal arrangements similar to marriage.

Ironically, the "Marriage Amendment", as it has come to be known, will affect common law marriages, and can eliminate benefits already given by businesses to same gender partners. It puts up yet another roadblock to prevent gay couples from receiving the legal protections of marriage and family law. Our newspapers, the *Dallas Morning News* and the *Ft. Worth Starr-Telegram*, have come out against this law. *The Dallas Morning News* called it inhumane.

I am preaching about it today because it affects us. Not only because we historically have defended human rights, but also because I am the one who represents this congregation in blessing these unions. I am preaching about it today because I want every marriage I bless to have the best possible odds of surviving. I'm preaching about it today because I believe the value of marriage should extend to all people.

I have continued to bless same gender marriages even after the Defense of Marriage act in 2003. I think the blessing of this congregation counts. But I have no illusions about its legal standing, and counsel same gender couples to take every legal step they can to assure they are protected.

This week, I received a poignant letter from one of our members about his experience when his partner of almost 25 years suddenly died. He was shut out of the emergency room; he was not allowed to make any decisions concerning his partner's body. He basically didn't exist, until a relative who understood the situation consulted with him.

When the partner of one of our members became ill and had to be taken to a nursing home, her family took all her possessions out of the house, effectively eradicating her presence in the home they had jointly-owned for many years. The loss of our member's partner was significant enough; the loss of what they had built together over decades was devastating.

This Constitutional Amendment threatens same-gender couples that have adopted children, as well. This amendment would make it harder for families to have any standing if any legal action were taken against them.

The irony of this amendment is that it also outlaws common law marriages that, until now, have had an historical basis that goes back to frontier days. Time was, that the circuit riding ministers and priests in Texas couldn't make it to a town but once or twice a year. So, couples were wedded when they declared themselves so—with the official duty being performed whenever the minister returned to town.

You may not know that in Texas, even now, if you present yourself as married, you are married (unless, of course, you are a same-gender couple). With the goal of 'defending marriage', this Constitutional Amendment will take away that stipulation.

It has been years since I officiated at my first Service of Union (or Wedding, as we now call them). I have learned over the years how very similar the values are which sustain both homosexual and heterosexual unions. Let me remind you of a few:

First, fidelity. If you haven't looked at the marriage vows lately, you may be surprised that (at least in this church) you promise that you will 'cling to no other'. And the vows are "till death do us part." The rings are a symbol of lots of things, but they are a sign to the world and a reminder to you that you are committed to another. It seems to me that we'd all be better off if we remembered that wedding rings are a sign of fidelity.

It's a struggle, this fidelity. I know it. But I also know that anyone who suggests that you'd be better off out of your marriage—so that you can be with them—does not have values worthy of you. If there is domestic violence or if other important values are not being respected, then the marriage may have to be dissolved. But an outside force shouldn't dissolve it. It's not worthy of your integrity.

Another moral value: "To love, honor, and cherish". We read earlier the chapter in I Corinthians on Love. It is hard to be consistently loving. It is hard to honor the other, when we want for ourselves. Cherishing is a tenderness, a holding lightly.

These spiritual qualities, grounded in moral behavior—for married people who intend to live together until death; who promise to love, honor and cherish one another; to create a home and a life together; to protect one another; to care for each other—are qualities we need more of, not something we need to restrict. And, although common law marriages have their problems, I will say that our frontier ancestors were right when they said that if you live married, you are married. Because marriage is a value built into the very fabric of our community. Families are good for children. Families are good for parents, and many helping hands are good for parents, too. The more our community supports families, and parents, and couples that have committed themselves to one another, the stronger our society can be.

It is not easy, this commitment. Ever. Whatever gender. Whatever the circumstances. It is not easy. But this is where the church comes in. This is where "love, honor, and cherish" comes in.

For, how do we become more authentic if we do not do it by becoming more human? And how do we become more human, if we live in judgment, or separation? How can we grow to be more authentic, if it is not in relation to other humans wanting the same, being formed by the same desires and hopes. To be loved, honored and cherished; to be safe, to be building something worth the investment of our lives. And how can we grow more authentic if we say that some of the people in our society must hide who they are, or even worse, whom they love. If we say they can't hold hands, or even imply that they are committed to each other?

There is a wonderful billboard on Highway 35E. It says, "Be careful, or the people you hate may turn out to be the people you love." It's a good 'talking point' for discussions with our friends and colleagues.

I look forward to the day when marriage will be legal for all adults in Texas; the day that our partners can be chosen freely and our commitments can be declared publicly. We'll all be the better for it. In the meantime, vote on November 6. And vote NO on Proposition 2.

 It's Christmas Because it's Dark
December 4, 2005

When Rick committed suicide, I thought for a long time that the church and I had failed him. I had no idea he was suicidal. His friends were stunned. It took years for me to be able to look back and see that perhaps he had lived longer than he would have alone, and also to see that it was our ritual observances of the season that got us all through. I haven't thought of ritual or of Christmas in the same way since. LH

Practicing the Scales of Rejoicing
By Richard Gilbert

We had forgotten how to sing until angel voices from mythical realms
of glory split the night with their song;
We had forgotten how dark and deep the night until the pure light of
    a birthing star opened our unseeing eyes.
We had forgotten the miracle of new life until some unknown poet
caught and sang the mystery.

How weary our step until the quickening holy day season.
How routine our stride before hearing a different song in the night.
How burdened with habit, now infused with time-honored freshness.

For the time being—eyes see a magical night of joy;
For the time being—ears hear melodies of the spirit over time's tumults;
For the time being—hearts comprehend what minds but dully grasp.

For the time being is all we have, we who are mortal flesh;
Somewhere between the triumphant night of birth and the dark day of
death we stand;
Somewhere between silence of beginning and the eternal deathless
silence of ending, we pause . . . .
For the time being is all we have for practicing the scales of rejoicing,
For singing into the dark and unknown night,
For flinging faithful tunes against the cold silence,
For beating rhythms of the soul over the cosmic cacophony,
For making melodies of meaning in the midst of senseless space,
For drawing from constricted voices sounds of joy despite all sadness,
For the time being is all we have for practicing the scales of rejoicing.[1]

There is a truth about Advent, a truth about Christmas, a truth about the
Solstice, a truth about Hanukkah that took me a long time to get. I learned it the

hard way—perhaps it was the only way. But it took me several years of being here in the church, practicing the joy of the season—one of my colleagues called it "Practicing the Scales of Rejoicing"—before I realized that something else was going on.

But I'm a little ahead of myself. Let me back up. Every year I hear it. Many years I say it: "This is just absurd! The way we rush around, buying gifts, mailing cards, rushing from event to event. It's a *terrible* season. Our expectations are always so high, we are inevitably disappointed. The intensity of it all is just too much. It causes too much pain. Why do we *do* this to ourselves?" There is so much darkness we feel because of Christmas. And it seems to be true. A Unitarian Universalist minister once told me that he always braces himself for the loss and grief of the season. "It's so hard," he said.

At first blush, it would seem that we should just be better organized; and for most of us, that would be true. How it is that every year (except for the one person who sent me a Christmas card that arrived this week and a few others of you who knew in July that this month would happen, who knew that December *would* come). Christmas always seems to come as a surprise. Resting from our Thanksgiving dinners, the month of Advent—in the Christian calendar a season of waiting for the holy child to arrive—almost inevitably comes to us as a shock.

We are now three weeks away from Christmas Day. If that doesn't strike fear in your hearts, I'm not sure what would. *Waiting*, indeed! If you don't think through what needs to be done *now*, you'll be in big trouble, because in three weeks it will be over.

I know it's become almost fashionable in some Unitarian Universalist circles to talk about skipping Christmas. The story is a myth, after all, in the sense that we're pretty sure it didn't happen as the story goes—and perhaps didn't even happen at all.

We know our country's obsession with shopping becomes voracious during this season. Everywhere we turn, we and our children are told to buy, buy, and buy. So, we talk about opting out of the shopping craze, or perhaps turning our gift giving to those especially in need. Or doing alternative shopping, devoting our resources to free trade coffee and cooperatively created items from undeveloped countries. Advent, a time of waiting and reflecting for many of us, turns into a time of resisting and deflecting the demands of the season.

This first Sunday in December is often the cusp, just before we begin the long mad slide into Christmas/Hanukkah/Solstice/Kwanzaa. The cusp where many of us resolve to not 'do' Christmas this year. Where many of us try to skip the parties, trim down the activities, perhaps not have a tree—maybe leave the decorations in their boxes. They'll be back in the closet in a month, anyway. Why not leave them there, because the demands of Christmas—which should be not only waiting and reflecting, but joy and light—are tough. So, we are tempted to skip it.

But I will tell you, you can't. Why? Because it's not up to you. There's something much bigger going on here, even for the disaffected and disinclined. Even for those who would declare Christmas a source of pain, debt, and ill will, to say nothing of the frenzy and sugar-highs of our children.

So, plan it out, if you wish.

Trim down the activities, if you must.

Don't get a tree, if it's too much to manage.

Skip the carol singing, if you want to.

But it won't change one iota the fact that *it's dark*.

I learned this one year when the trees *were* decorated, the plans made, the cards sent, Hanging of the Greens planned, and the Christmas Eve services well in hand. I learned it when I had scheduled visits to shut ins, had thought through the Christmas story as it comes down to us—with the miracle of Jesus' birth and the sky filled with the Glory of God. And then, one of my favorite people in the church committed suicide.

It turns out that his death would not be the only suicide at Christmas I would experience. Nor would it be the only death. And I am not, because of my particular role in this church community, the only one who experiences these things. It turns out that death comes close this time of year, inexplicably, even with all our medical advances, even with what we know. Death comes close in this season.

And we, no different from our ancestors, feel it, know it. When we drive to work in the dark and drive home from work in the dark, even with all our electricity, deep at the core of things our hearts and minds remember the darkness of all time, and what it took to survive. That year, the first time I was flattened at Christmas by an unthinkable tragedy, I learned it:

It's not dark because it's Christmas; it's Christmas because it's dark.

That year I barely made it through singing carols, having to write down the addresses of all my friends across the land and send them notes of greeting, having to go to church and be with babies and couples about to be married, being forced to go to pot lucks and exchange gifts, and make phone calls to distant relatives, and decorate a tree—all of it demanded by our culture. All of it I did that year on automatic, without vision—even without hope—and it turned out to be what got me through. Because, more than anything else—more than waiting, more than reflection, more than all our preparations—this season is a season in which we are called to face the darkness head-on, and sing anyway.

I believe that beyond the Search for the Historical Jesus, beyond the Jesus Seminar, beyond the skills of Biblical Criticism I learned in seminary, beyond even whether we are Christian, Jew, Moslem, Buddhist, or don't even care; beyond all the overlays of traditional religion, this story of a baby born against all odds, in paradoxical circumstances, this story of a child born in the dark, in a stable, is a story, simply, of hope.

We tell it because the darkness is deep.

The Carols are songs of joy. We sing them because the darkness is deep.
The Candles are such little lights. We light them because the darkness is deep.
Our national potlatch requires that we give. We give gifts because the darkness is deep.
And we come here, to sing, to tell the stories, to light the candles, to give our gifts—
Because the darkness is deep.

W.H. Auden, early in his Christmas Oratorio, *For the Time Being,*[2] says in a stunning passage that takes us more deeply into the reality of things:

> If, on account of the political situation,
> There are quite a number of homes without roofs, and men
> Lying about in the countryside neither drunk, nor asleep,
>   . . .
> If it's unwise now to say much in letters, and if,
> Under the subnormal temperatures prevailing,
> The two sexes are at present the weak and the strong,
>   This is not at all unusual for this time of year.
>   . . .
> Till lately we knew of no other, and between us we seemed
> To have what it took—the adrenal courage of the tiger,
> The chameleon's discretion, the modesty of the doe,
> Or the fern's devotion to spatial necessity:
> To practice one's peculiar civic virtue was not
> So impossible after all; to cut our losses
> And bury our dead was really quite easy: That was why
> We were always able to say: "We are children of God,
> And our Father has never forsaken His people.
>   But then we were children.

The remainder of Auden's oratorio goes on to describe the Christmas story in gripping poetry as the fulfillment of our demand, as adults, for a miracle, knowing that nothing can save us from death. Every time I read Auden's description of our time, I think it is uncanny. His deft wordsmithing of despair is worth our re-visit every season of darkness.

It is easy to get caught up in this rendering of the Christmas story, powerfully, in the voices of the people given shape and dimension. This is no nostalgic trip through Christmases past. This is a journey through political and personal reality, interwoven with the deep archetypal story of the babe born in a manger and scooped up to head to Egypt so he wouldn't be killed by Herod.

The awful truth of December is that nothing is settled. Death is real. *And so is birth.*

For those of us temporarily able to celebrate, and that would be all of us, I might add. For those of us who are alive this Christmas, in this dark season. For those of us who don't know if we will be back next year, and none of us do know that. For those of us who have found ourselves in darkness, on account of the political situation—Auden said—or, on a more personal basis, quite simply because we've noticed . . . It's dark.

For those of us who are grieving (and I don't think there are many outside this category), who have been disappointed, perhaps even betrayed. For those of us who have been cast out, perhaps from our childhood, when we believed we were safe. For those of us who have tasted fear. For all of us who know that darkness is not only a fact of our lives, but a quality of eternity.

For us does the light shine. For us is the song sung. For us does the birth of a babe in a manger serve as a reminder that hope smiles back even when we are weary. Reminds us again of love and calls us to the practices of the season.

It's not dark because it's Christmas. It's Christmas because it's dark. Submit yourselves to its calls to be together, to sing loudly, to tell the story incessantly, to be more generous than you can imagine, and to love one another.

 It's About the Theology
August 27, 2006

Sometimes when people find out that we have no prescribed beliefs they think it means we don't have any beliefs. The opposite is true. It is important in our church that people pay attention to their beliefs, and live them. Unitarian minister Wallace Robbins once said, "We will not be restrained in our beliefs." It's true. LH

Excerpt from *The Free Mind*
By William Ellery Channing

I call that mind free which masters the senses, and which recognizes its own reality and greatness; which passes life, not in asking what it shall eat or drink, but in hungering, thirsting, and seeking after righteousness.

I call that mind free which jealously guards its intellectual rights and powers, which does not content itself with a passive or hereditary faith; which opens itself to light whensoever it may come, which receives new truth as an angel from heaven.

I call that mind free which is not passively framed by outward circumstances, and is not the creature of accidental impulse; which discovers everywhere the radiant signatures of the infinite spirit, and in them finds help to its own spiritual enlargement.

I call that mind free which protects itself against the usurpations of society, and which does not cower to human opinion; which refuses to be the slave or tool of the many or of the few, and guards its empire over itself as nobler than the empire of the world.

I call that mind free which resists the bondage of habit, which does not mechanically copy the past, nor live on its old virtues; but which listens for new and higher monitions of conscience, and rejoices to pour itself forth in fresh and higher exertions.

I call that mind free which sets no bounds to its love, which wherever they are seen, delights in virtue and sympathizes with suffering; which recognizes in all human beings the image of God and the rights of God's children, and offers itself up a willing sacrifice in the cause of humankind.

I call that mind free which has cast off all fear but that of wrongdoing, and which no menace or peril can enthrall; which is calm in the midst of tumults, and possesses itself, though all else be lost. [1]

I Corinthians 13: 1-8

> If I speak in the tongues of men and of angels, but have not love,
> I am a noisy gong or a clanging cymbal.
> And if I have prophetic powers, and understand all mysteries
> and all knowledge, and if I have all faith, so as to remove mountains,
> but have not love, I am nothing.
> If I give away all I have, and if I deliver my body to be burned,
> but have not love, I gain nothing.
> Love is patient and kind; love is not jealous or boastful; it is not
> arrogant or rude. Love does not insist on its own way; it is not irritable
> or resentful; it does not rejoice at wrong, but rejoices in the right.
> Love bears all things, believes all things, hopes all things,
> endures all things. Love never ends . . .

My brother told me recently that he had been invited to church by one of his co-workers. He said it was a beautiful church, with many in attendance. He said the "production values" couldn't have been better. (He's an engineer; that would be something he would notice.) They had small groups, and he went to one of their gatherings—at Stern Grove in San Francisco for an outdoor concert and afterwards to the home of a member of the church for coffee and conversation—which he thoroughly enjoyed. He then said, "It took me a month before I realized that the theology was terrible."

Now, my brother and I were raised in a Fundamentalist church. We have both left. He was active for a time in a Presbyterian Church in Seattle, and then—when he and his family moved to Mountain View, on the Peninsula south of San Francisco—he dropped that affiliation and has since enjoyed the "church of sleeping in," the "church of bicycle club tours," the "church of going to work and catching up," and the "church of outdoor fairs and events", of which there are many where he lives. He has dabbled in a Unitarian Universalist Church in his area, but found it rather ingrown. And, now, when invited, he will attend church with a friend. So this was a new version of an old quest.

I assume at least some of you are here today with a similar itch. You are wanting to find a place for your family, for your life. Wanting to find a place that gives you solace as well as challenge, nurture as well as offering reminders of important values to live by. A community for your family, religious education for your children. A place to live your life through all the inevitable changes—the joy as well as the grief. I assume some of you are here today, perhaps for the first time, with similar, perhaps unspoken hopes for what you will find here. Let me say this: it all starts with the theology.

Most people these days don't put theology at the top of their list of what they are looking for in a church. Or at least they don't think they do. Like my brother, they see a church as a whole—as a community, as a Sunday morning experience—but have long ago abandoned concerns about doctrinal truth. Perhaps even forgetting that if they were once in a church (as my brother and I were), they left it (as we did) for theological reasons. Theology seems too much like a dusty topic for boring classrooms, having little to do with a vibrant, active involved church that can help you live your life with purpose and meaning.

But let me say here at the outset that it's *all* about the theology. Once people realize that the "production values" (the programs, the small groups) of a church are the vehicle, not the message, they understand that the theology is what is important as we teach our children, as we do our good works in the world—as we find the very meaning of our lives.

So let me start with Love—a theology of love. This is not the "all you need is love" of the Beatles, although that is a good place to start. It is the love that Hosea Ballou read about in the late 1700's in his Bible, just as we read this morning from I Corinthians. As the story goes, Hosea Ballou, the son of a hellfire and brimstone Baptist minister, read his Bible out behind the barn after his chores were done. He came to the conclusion that the God found there was a God of love. And if God was a God of love, if God was a loving Father (God was only a 'He' back then), he would not send anyone to hell.

Young Hosea Ballou grew up to be a preacher himself. At one point in our nation's history, he was part of the third largest denominational body in the country. They called themselves Universalists, and centered their beliefs on a loving God. Not that humans don't sin. Not that we're all just lovely and there is no need to worry about ethics, or the harm we do to one another and to our world. Not that. But rather, the belief that humans—in all our frailty, in all our fallibility, even in our out-and-out selfishness and injustice—have access to forgiveness deeper than we can even imagine.

What this means is that if someone asks you if you are saved, you can say without reservation or qualification, "Yes." Because you are. Always have been and always will be. It means "no hell" (except perhaps the hell we manage to create here, right now, on earth). That simple historical theological idea turns most of what stands for religion on its head. We don't have to parse out believer from unbeliever, acceptable from unacceptable, saved from damned, worthy from unworthy.

Now I will admit that it also means that we can't count on God for final retribution for sins against humanity. It does take away the idea that, in the end, God will even things out. And it does mean that we have to struggle with putting love and justice together in a very real world of hate and injustice. And *that's* not easy. But I only promised you a theology today, not necessarily an easy one.

James Luther Adams was a Unitarian theologian who came of age during the Nazi buildup in Germany. He was a theological student, and before he fled back to America he saw with his own eyes the failure of the church in the face of growing evil. He also saw a few instances of great bravery and sacrifice. His theology was never the same. From that point forward in his young life, Adams (I heard him speak of his experiences in the later years of his career, which had spanned decades of teaching at the University of Chicago and Harvard Divinity School) taught that beliefs only have meaning as they are embodied in your life and in the life of institutions.

Beliefs are not something you decide, he said, they are embedded in your life. Beliefs are not statements chiseled in stone to be recited each week in church, they are the core out of which we live. Beliefs are found in the struggles of our time and in our responses. They are found in the ways we use our resources, in the ways we treat each other, and in the ways we live. Beliefs are not beliefs until we *live* them, he said, as individuals and in our communities and in the structures of our society.

And so when we say, "It's about the theology," we don't mean doctrine about whether women should speak in church. We don't mean whether gay men and lesbians and transgender people are loved by God. We don't mean who should or shouldn't be ministers. We don't mean who God has chosen or not chosen. We don't mean which rituals are allowed to be partaken by whom. We don't mean prescriptions about how God has arranged the world and the hereafter. We don't even mean to describe who God is, and who God listens to, and how to get God to do what we want.

Historically, what has come down to us from people who, like us, struggle with how to live deeply within the purposes of love and justice? What has come down to us is this: our knowledge of things, what we would call truth, is always partial—significant, but always partial. We have learned to be suspicious of people who say, "God wants this" or "God says that" knowing that any one perception of ultimate truth or personal insight is always partial.

Because our perception of truth is partial, we need one another. (We need one another for lots of reasons, but I'm talking about theology today.) And when we 'get it' that our experience, our insight, our understanding of meaning and purpose—what some call the action of God in the world—is always partial, then being together becomes crucial because *you* can enlarge *my* understanding, and maybe *I* can enlarge *yours*. Not only of how we think about things, but also of how to live. When I see someone living sacrificially, living truthfully, living his or her life with purpose, it helps me find my own place, my own strength, and my own way.

Back when I was 22 and new to the Unitarian Universalist church, I used to read the "Letters to the Editor" written by members of the church to the local paper and posted on our bulletin board. I admired the people who wrote those letters. I imagined someday I would write letters to the editor. I recognized by that simple witness that being a Unitarian Universalist meant you were active in your community. It meant that you found your own voice and used it. I learned that early on in my church.

And I learned that belief in the Trinity was too limiting. That the names of God as Father, Son, and Holy Spirit are helpful, but not enough. That the church is a place to report our own experiences of God. A place to try to find words that speak to the deep realities of our lives, the names and the silence that goes deeper than names. Never stopping the process of listening, paying attention, and speaking aloud about our experience of life, even when it isn't pretty. And knowing always that it is insufficient. Ralph Waldo Emerson, for part of his life a Unitarian minister and for all his life a seeker of truth, said, "When the half-gods go, the gods arrive."[2]

Naming and renaming, seeing and then seeing more clearly. Understanding and then not understanding, and then perhaps understanding again in a new way. Looking with new eyes each day at this gift that is ours, as life comes to us with its surprises, its challenges, even its grief, but also its joy. This is the theology worth living. With its ever-fresh sense of how it is with us, with the world, with life.

Two more points, and then I will stop.

Suffering isn't punishment for what we've done. Suffering is part of life itself. Knowing this can liberate us and help us be more compassionate with ourselves and with others. We are not separate from those who suffer. It's important to know that.

And it's important to know that religion is about *this* life, not some later life. Stick around long enough and you will hear some of us wonder about what happens when we die. I know that what we think about the hereafter does affect how we live. But religion can't tell us about the next life. It can only tell us about this one. If you believe that, you will also know that we can't expect justice to wait for another time and place, love to fulfill itself somewhere else, or peace to come when all is done in this life.

There is much more to be said. If you are visiting today I hope you will feel you have been welcomed. At least when someone says, "Oh, those Unitarian Universalists don't have any beliefs," you can say, "yes they do," deeply embedded in their history and their lives. If you want to learn more, stick around. Look at the newsletter. See if we practice what we preach. Maybe this will be your church home too.

Work It Out
May 13, 2007

This was fun to preach. There is so much we have to simply work out. Perhaps it is more accurate to say, stand back while it works out. It's especially gratifying to see that, most of the time, it does . . . work out. LH

Excerpt from *On Being Mom*
By Anna Quindlen

If not for the photographs, I might have a hard time believing they ever existed. The pensive infant with the swipe of dark bangs and the black button eyes of a Raggedy Andy doll. The placid baby with the yellow ringlets and the high piping voice. The sturdy toddler with the lower lip that curled into an apostrophe above her chin.

All my babies are gone now. I say this not in sorrow but in disbelief. I take great satisfaction in what I have today: three almost-adults, two taller than I am, one closing in fast. Three people who . . . miraculously, go to the bathroom, zip up their jackets and move food from plate to mouth all by themselves. Like the trick soap I bought for the bathroom with a rubber ducky at its center, the baby is buried deep within each, barely discernible except through the unreliable haze of the past.

Everything in all the books I once pored over is finished for me now. Penelope Leach, T. Berry Brazelton, Dr. Spock. The ones on sibling rivalry and sleeping through the night and early-childhood education, all grown obsolete. Along with *Goodnight Moon* and *Where the Wild Things Are,* they are battered, spotted, well used. But I suspect that if you flipped the pages dust would rise like memories.

What those books taught me, finally, and what the women on the playground taught me, and the well-meaning relations—what they taught me, was that they couldn't really teach me very much at all. Raising children is presented at first as a true-false test, then becomes multiple choice, until finally, far along, you realize that it is an endless essay. No one knows anything. One child responds well to positive reinforcement, another can be managed only with a stern voice and a timeout. One child is toilet trained at 3, his sibling at 2. When my first child was born, parents were told to put baby to bed on his belly so that he would not choke on his own spit-up. By the time my last arrived, babies were put down on their backs because of research on sudden infant death syndrome. To a new parent this ever-shifting certainty is terrifying, and then soothing.

Eventually you must learn to trust yourself. Eventually the research will follow. I remember 15 years ago poring over one of Dr. Brazelton's wonderful books on child development, in which he describes three different sorts of infants; average, quiet, and active. I was looking for a sub-quiet codicil for an 18-month-old who did not walk. Was there something wrong with his fat little legs? Was there something wrong with his tiny little mind? Was he developmentally delayed, physically challenged? Was I insane? Last year he went to China. Next year he goes to college. He can talk just fine. He can walk, too. Every part of raising children is humbling, too. Believe me, mistakes were made. They have all been enshrined in the, "Remember-When-Mom-Did Hall of fame." The outbursts, the temper tantrums, the bad language, mine, not theirs. The times the baby fell off the bed. The times I arrived late for preschool pickup. The nightmare sleepover. The horrible summer camp. The day when the youngest came barreling out of the classroom with a 98 on her geography test, and I responded, "What did you get wrong?: . . . The time I ordered food at the McDonald's drive-through speaker and then drove away without picking it up from the window . . . I did not allow them to watch the Simpsons for the first two seasons. What was I thinking? . . .

The books said to be relaxed and I was often tense, matter-of-fact and I was sometimes over the top. And look how it all turned out. I wound up with the three people I like best in the world, who have done more than anyone to excavate my essential humanity. That's what the books never told me. I was bound and determined to learn from the experts. It just took me awhile to figure out who the experts were.[1]

I want to tell you about my glory moment in parenting. There are two or three, but this one stands out as having perfect timing, the perfect amount of direction. It was actually, in retrospect, one of the wisest moments of all my years parenting my son. I have one son, now 37, so I have lots of eggs in one basket, and have for a long time.

As is true of many experiences in life, our best moments are often our most inadvertent moments. And so, unfortunately, I can't claim it as having come from my deep store of wisdom about parenting. I tell it to you because I was at the end of my rope. I was fairly new in Dallas, without long term friendships there, and with the usual stresses of starting a ministry in a new church. Several events had occurred in my family which had added to the stress. My days were what some of us have called 'suit up and show up' days, when you don't have a lot to give, but you give anyway.

I tell you all this as background to my most glorious moment of parenting. One day during this difficult time, I was standing at the sink washing dishes when my son walked in behind me. He said from the doorway of the kitchen, "I've decided I won't go to college this year." I can remember this as if it were yesterday. I stopped, without turning, and thought "I can't handle this. I don't have any way to handle this."

And I turned around and said, "Work it out." He started to argue with me, then stopped mid-sentence, realizing I hadn't argued with him. Startled, he said "okay." He called the University where he had been admitted and postponed his admission for a year.

He later told me that he didn't feel up to it. So I arranged for him to have a checkup. The doctor said he couldn't find anything wrong, that perhaps it was just some malaise from coming back to the States. So, my son then followed part of his original plan and moved to Minnesota, where his father lived.

Three weeks later, after a harrowing period of trying to figure out what was wrong with him, he was finally diagnosed with tuberculosis—picked up somewhere during his wide-ranging travels. So, he was right. He shouldn't have started college that fall. At the time, he just didn't know *why*. And I was right to tell him to work it out.

The next few months, it was strange to have to hope that he was following the strict treatment regimen he had to follow to get well. I remain grateful to my son's step-mother for caring for him when I couldn't. He did get well. Fortunately, when you're in generally good health and you're young, tuberculosis can be simply something you get through. He has no apparent scars on his lungs and has had no recurrence.

But I will tell you, I learned a lot from that day. Of course, you know that I'm not telling you it's the only response to give a child. There are times you do have to figure out what needs to happen. But I know that at that particular moment—because I *couldn't* help, or analyze or suggest, or argue back—I was able to put the ball firmly in his court. Because I didn't have the resources to do otherwise, it was the right response at the right moment.

There is an interesting epilogue to that story. The following year, when he did enter the University, he became an outstanding student. His grades up to then had been fair, and then only if a course captured his interest. When I commented on his stellar career in college, as compared to his less than stellar career in high school, his reply was, "Well, mom, you know I almost died."

Now, I wouldn't wish that on anyone's children. But having been through the valley, he claimed his own life. *If* you live to tell the story, you are never the same. And if you are 17 or 18, that is extraordinarily life shaping. I think what happened that day in the kitchen of the Parsonage was a clear passing of the mantle of responsibility.

If I back up and think over the whole of his life, I remember other times when the ball was in his court. The time we walked into his nursery school, and he inexplicably balked and wouldn't let me leave. For once I had the good sense to sit down on the floor in the corner with him until we could figure out what was wrong. (There are other not so stellar moments, when I was in a rush to get to work, that I won't share today). But *that* day, I sat down.

It turned out that we both knew his nursery school was moving to a different building a couple of blocks away. That day—the part I didn't realize—someone had donated moving boxes to begin the packing. Seeing the boxes, Peter assumed they were moving that day and suddenly wasn't sure I would know where to find him when school was over. It took a while, but finally I was able to assure him that I would be back there that day, because they weren't moving that day. And that when they did move, I already knew where the new school would be. So I could find him. He was okay, and ran off to play with his friends.

This being human, and giving birth to humans, is tricky business. Anna Quindlen was right when she said we are so bound and determined to learn from the experts. But, in her essay it's a little ambiguous as to who she thought the experts were. Was she the expert? Were her children? My answer would be both. For, in all relationships in life, we have to be our own experts and then look to the other as an expert with a different point of view. If either the parent or the child is left out of the equation, things can easily go awry.

I have lived through whole theories of child-centered parenting. I grew up with parent-centered parenting. It seems obvious to me now that parents need to know all there is to know about the development and limitations of their children (they are children, after all) *and* be parents. Children need parents. More than anything else, to protect them, to guide them, to put limits on them, to help them make good choices—no matter how harrowing the job becomes. And at the same time—and this is the difficult part, because it is *at the same time*—parents need to look to their *children* as their primary resource for the information they need.

I was the one who took a shopping bag full of birthing books to the hospital when I was in labor with my son. When something unexpected occurred, I would ask my husband to look it up. We were the most well informed parents on the floor. At one point someone asked me if I was a nurse! But that baby was born in God's own time, and all the books in the world couldn't have prepared me for that experience. I only realized in retrospect that it would be a model for the rest of our lives. At least so far.

Yesterday, I received a letter from my brother's granddaughter. She is graduating from college next month and planning to marry next year. She sent a long handwritten letter (she apologized for not being able to do a spell-check on it since it was handwritten.)

In the letter she referred to a visit she and her brother and mother made to my home. They came here to church while they were visiting. Four years later, she writes to me, "Intelligent and tolerant people are kind of hard to find . . . so it was refreshing and relieving to see that it existed in my genetics." She went on to explain that she and her fiancé are what I would call spiritual, but not religious. She said that friends have tried the Unitarian Universalist church near them and found it a 'less than stellar experience.' She asked me to officiate at their wedding, which I will be honored to do.

The truth is, she is not the only religious liberal in her family, even if she doesn't count me. And I believe she needs a *church* as much as she needs a spiritual path. It also isn't a good idea to have the wedding and reception simultaneously, as she suggests. But, you know what? She's going to have to work it out.

Of course, I will tell her and her fiancé what I know about weddings and marriage. I will gently ask them some important questions. But I will honor what I consider to be a sacred space between us. It exists between Mother and Son, Mother and Daughter, and in this case Great-Aunt and Grand-Niece (we'll get to Fathers next month). It exists between friends and between spouses when, instead of moving into a situation, we are called to back up, to let the other person learn something important about life.

In parenting circles when I was a young parent and teacher, we called it "logical consequences". Sometimes it's hard to bear, but letting life unfold, even if it is painful, is sometimes the best parenting of all. Backing up, saying "work it out," watching from afar, teaching them to trust their own instincts—even when we're not sure *we* do—can be better by far than never letting them try their own wings.

So, if you've managed to make it to adulthood—whether through the good graces of loving parents, or the blessings of people you rarely saw, but thought of as models for your life—today is a day to be grateful. If you are a mother, you and I (with Anna Quinlan) can all admit that mistakes have been made. But we can still let our children work it out. Because the space between us is God space, it is life space; it is territory that is sacred. It has a timeframe that is much more spacious than our pressured minutes, days and months. It has purpose that goes much farther even than our own lives and meaning deeper than we can ever know.

Work it out is not only a strategy, it is a gift. A Mothers' Day gift. To all of us. All our days.

Forgiveness
February 3, 2008

I learned a lot, preaching this sermon. This was one of those sermons that ended up in a different place than I had planned. It's a cliché, but still true, that preachers often preach what we need most to hear ourselves. LH

From *My Grandfather's Blessings*
By Rachel Naomi Remen

Many years ago, I was invited to hear a well-known rabbi speak about forgiveness at a Yom Kippur service. Yom Kippur is the Day of Atonement, when Jews everywhere reflect on the year just past, repent their shortcomings and unkindness, and hope for the forgiveness of God. But the rabbi did not speak about God's forgiveness.

Instead, he walked out into the congregation, took his infant daughter from his wife, and, carrying her in his arms, stepped up to the bimah or podium. The little girl was perhaps a year old and she was adorable. From her father's arms she smiled at the congregation. Every heart melted. Turning toward her daddy, she patted him on the cheek with her tiny hands. He smiled fondly at her and with his customary dignity began a rather traditional Yom Kippur sermon, talking about the meaning of the holiday.

The baby girl, feeling his attention shift away from her, reached forward and grabbed his nose. Gently he freed himself and continued the sermon. After a few minutes, she took his tie and put it in her mouth. The entire congregation chuckled. She put her tiny arms around his neck. Looking at us over the top of her head, he said, "Think about it. Is there anything she can do that you could not forgive her for?" . . .

Just then she reached up and grabbed his eyeglasses. Everyone laughed out loud.

Retrieving his eyeglasses and settling them on his nose, the rabbi laughed as well. Still smiling, he waited for silence. When it came, he asked, "And when does that stop? When does it get hard to forgive? At three? At seven? A t fourteen? At thirty-five? How old does someone have to be before you forget that everyone is a child of God?"

Back then, God's forgiveness was something easily understandable to me, but personally I found forgiveness difficult. I had thought of it as a lowering of standards rather than a family relationship.[1]

From *The Spirituality of Imperfection*
By Ernest Kurtz and Katherine Ketcham

> A former inmate of a Nazi concentration camp was visiting a friend who had shared the ordeal with him.
> "Have you forgiven the Nazis?" he asked his friend.
> "Yes."
> "Well, I haven't. I'm still consumed with hatred for them."
> "In that case," said his friend gently, "they still have you in prison."[2]

Today I want to talk about forgiveness as a state of being, rather than what you do when someone has wronged you. But of course we have to start with what you do when someone has wronged you.

It starts with what I can only call a 'hairball'. I have called it, over the years, "the generational grudge" or "leftovers" from a relationship gone bad. It is as small as unfairness at work and as large as systemic oppression. Whatever its source, it catches you by surprise, or makes you function in denial, using up psychological and spiritual space. However you know or feel it, it's a knot, a frozen place deep in the heart and soul that won't budge.

We can decide to forgive—consciously 'turn the other cheek', as we are taught in the Christian scriptures. Or forgive "not seven times, but seventy times seven times", as when Peter asks Jesus how often he had to forgive his brother (suggesting seven times might be a possible limit).

What has come from Jesus' answer to Peter seems to be a belief in Christianity that the ideal is that we allow ourselves to be misused, mistreated, and maligned *ad infinitum*. As long as it takes.

"Always turn the other cheek" seems to be the message. At least it was the one I got, growing up. Certainly a step forward from the "eye for an eye, and tooth for a tooth" which runs deep in our world and, these days, across our television screens. But, in the face of abuse and hatred and the need for all of us to take our rightful place in the world, "always turning the other cheek" is an odd doctrine

This race for the Presidency of the Unitarian Universalist Association has brought me into situations that I have not had to experience before. I find myself encountering odd assumptions about who I am and what I believe.

I met with the Executive Committee of a group in our denomination about something I had done (long before I entered the race for President which, as you know, began January 1st of this year). I worked hard to understand their concerns. I listened. I knew I was the learner in the situation, because I had opinions (of course!), but wanted to hear their perspective. I tried to be as truthful and authentic as I could be. (I do recommend this kind of attention when confronted by someone's judgment: at least start by hearing him or her out.)

After much discussion, I said—somewhat to my own surprise—"I'm sorry that happened. I could have managed that whole situation much better than I did. But I'm afraid I have to say that going forward in this campaign, I know I will screw up again. I'm glad I know you better and I know we have a basis for working things out. But I also know I will screw up again. In fact . . . I'd like to apologize now, ahead of time, for those times when I screw up again."

By that time we had cleared the air enough, and they laughed. We parted with a good basis for our relationship going forward in our common struggles.

I've thought a lot about that day since then. Because as soon as the words came out of my mouth, I realized that the idea was new for me. "I am going to screw up. It goes with the territory. It's part of this adventure."

What up until then had felt like a push to be better, do better, get better, *not* screw up, had become the rather liberating realization that especially in the rough and tumble world of running for President of the UUA, I'm going to screw up. I will say the wrong thing. I will do the wrong thing. I will fall short of my own hopes and the hopes of others. And, I am also going to articulate the realities of our faith in our time, with the goal of helping the people who deeply care about our faith find a new way to understand what is possible.

But, back to falling short. Admitting that I knew I would, freed us all, but especially *me*. For of course, what *is* forgiveness if we ask for forgiveness forward?

Now I know my audience today. You're not likely to consider "asking for forgiveness forward" as a *carte blanche* to do what you want, no matter how hurtful.

No, I know who you are. If you came because of the title of the sermon, it might be because you were hoping for some handle, some way to access the ability to forgive. Perhaps even the unforgivable. And it may seem odd to think that the path to forgiving might be, at least in part, the ability to know that you (like me) will screw up and need forgiveness, going forward—and that caring about the relationships where that forgiveness will be needed is a beginning.

I believe this is at the core of our life together here at the church. If we have made any progress on issues of gender, sexual identity, race—or problems of simply living together as families and friends—it will begin with the acknowledgement that we *will* screw up and we *will* need forgiveness. It will begin with that liberating knowledge. Only then will we be able to see our way clear to change our behavior.

Second point. If you can't forgive, you are still in bondage. That's a funny thing about forgiving: it is largely letting go. Not that we haven't been damaged. Not that it doesn't matter. Not that what has happened isn't painful. We have been damaged. There is not a person here who hasn't been scarred by others. It is painful. It is not fair.

But, the starting place for forgiveness is to remember *that that was then and this is now.* If you carry those grudges, if you nurse your wounds, if you rail at the unfairness of your situation, you will be in bondage to that person, that event, long after it is over. And it is even possible to get in the habit of accumulating grudges and wounds and have them be so much a part of the fabric of our lives that we can't even see when changes have occurred, or the grudge isn't worth it any more. More than once I have heard from people that they were so resentful they hadn't noticed a change in another person. And when they did notice, they were thrown into the realization that maybe they needed to change. Life does go on, after all, and people do change. It's best to keep that possibility at least in your back pocket, so you don't miss it when it occurs.

Like the man who was asked by a fellow Holocaust survivor whether he had forgiven the Nazis, he said, "I am consumed with hatred for them". His friend replied, "In that case, they still have you in prison."

I can't say this more emphatically. As long as you carry hatred and resentment over things past, you are still in it. You are missing today because of yesterday. Give it up.

Point 3. This caught me by surprise: Rachel Naomi Remen's comment in her book about forgiveness being difficult for her because she had always thought of it as a lowering of standards, rather than a family relationship.

Certainly this is a tension in raising children. How do we encourage behavior that will help our children grow into happy, functioning adults? How can we provide a structured, secure environment for them? How can we communicate our belief in them, our hopes for them, without creating standards of behavior? And how does forgiveness become part of that process? Or should it? These are questions I struggled with all the time my son was growing up. As a single parent, it was hard to be the loving, affirming parent, and at the same time introduce him to developmentally appropriate civility.

I got it, when I read Rachel Naomi Remen's short sentence: I had thought of forgiveness as a lowering of standards rather than a family relationship. Forgiveness is not one act. It is a relationship. I remember saying to my son, "I'd like to do that one over." Sometimes I had overreacted; sometimes I hadn't really communicated what I meant. Sometimes I just wanted to back up and be clear about what I knew he needed to know.

That habit of wanting to do-over, in a calmer moment—I didn't realize it then, but I do now—was a way of putting what had happened in context. In a relationship. And it was the relationship that was forgiving.

So what about strife worldwide? What about not only generational grudges, but also ethnic and tribal bitterness? It is a luxury to preach, "turn the other cheek" if your children are starving or in danger of being killed at any moment in ethnic violence. Do these principles hold?

Remembering: We will always need forgiving . . . Asking for forgiveness forward . . . Realizing that forgiveness is not lowering one's standards, but participating in a relationship . . . Do these principles hold on a global level? Not so well, it seems. We do have models. William F. Vendley, the Secretary General of Religions for Peace, says that, in difficult negotiations he always starts with the children. People can move forward in negotiations when they can remember the children. In South Africa, Bishop Tutu has provided a model of reconciliation that includes confessions of atrocities heard by the victims—empowering both victims and perpetrators to be full participants in the society going forward. Our own Lee Taft is working on forgiveness in medical, legal, and governmental wrongs, not only as an alternative to expensive litigation, but also as a way to healing.

Human beings are capable of great harm, both intentionally and as the result of unintended consequences. We now have to consider what forgiveness will look like when generations who follow us will wonder why we ignored the ecological crisis at our doorstep.

When we finally realize that forgiveness is not a lowering of standards and that we'll need it all our lives, as will those we love, then we may be equipped to practice forgiveness in larger ways. Becoming the hearts and hands of the forgiving one, 70 times 70 times, until our opportunity to forgive and ask forgiveness ends.

 Bibliography

Is God a Christian?

1. Rilke, Rainer Maria. *You, Neighbor God*. Poems from the Book of Hours. New Directions, New York, 1941.
2. Dillard, Annie. Teaching a Stone to Talk, Revised Edition. Harper Perennial, New York, 1988.
2. Finneran, Richard J., editor. The Collected Works of W. B. Yeats, Volume 1. Scribner, New York, 1997.

Cheap Grace

1. Bonhoeffer, Dietrich. *Sorrow and Joy*. Prisoner for God: Letters and Papers from Prison. The Macmillan Company, New York, 1953.
2. Gibran, Kahlil. The Prophet. Alfred A. Knopf, New York. 1968.
3. Pauck, Wilhelm, editor. Lectures on Romans. Westminister Press, Philadelphia, 1961.

When the Half Gods Go

1. Emerson, Ralph Waldo. *Give all to love*. Early Poems of Ralph Waldo Emerson. Thomas Y. Crowell & Company, New York, 1899.

Practice Resurrection

1. Berry, Wendell. *Manifesto: The Mad Farmer Liberation Front*. The Country of Marriage. Harcourt Brace, New York, 1973.

Like a Pool into Which We Plunge

1. Dunn, Richard and Laetitia Yaendle, editors. The Journal of John Winthrop,1630-1649. President and Fellows of Harvard College and the Massachusetts Historical Society, Canada, 1996.
2. Lawrence, D.H. *There Are No Gods*. Collected Poems. Jonathan Cape and Harrison Smith, New York, 1928.
3. Rich, Adrienne. *Diving into the Wreck*. The Fact of a Doorframe: Selected Poems 1950-2001. W.W. Norton and Co., New York, 2002.

It Has Made All the Difference

1. Rankin, David. *All Beliefs* from The Unitarian Universalist Pocket Guide. Harry Scholefield, ed. Unitarian Universalist Association, 1981.
2. McLean, Angus. The Wind in both Ears. Unitarian Universalist Association Press, 1987.

The Good Marriage

1. Moore, Thomas. Soul Mates. Harper Collins, New York, 1994.

Mother Earth and Father God

1. Mitchell, Stephen. A Book of Psalms. Harper Collins, New York, 1993.
2. Roberts, Elizabeth and Elias Amidon. Earth Prayers Around the World. Harper, San Francisco, 1991.
3. Gaster, Theodore. Festivals of the Jewish Year. Morrow Quill Paperbacks, New York, 1978.

Why I am a Rational Mystic

1. Ahlstrom, Sydney and Jonathan Carey, eds. An American Reformation: A Documentary History of Unitarian Christianity. Wesleyan University Press, Middletown, CT, 1985.
2. Ibid.
3. Emerson. *Harvard Divinity School Address*, July 15, 1838.
4. Job 38:1, 4, 6b, 7.
5. Job 38: 8, 9.

God's Wild Card

1. Sexton, Anne. *The Rowing Endeth*. The Awful Rowing Toward God. Houghton Mifflin Company, Boston, 1975.
2. Chesterton, G.K. Orthodoxy. Barnes and Noble, New York, 2007.

How to Help Your Child Have a Spiritual Life

1. Fahs, Sophia Blanche Lyon. *It Matters What We Believe*. Papers. Andover Harvard Library, Harvard Divinity School, Cambridge, bMS 72/20/30.
2. Gibran, Kahlil. The Prophet. Alfred A. Knopf, New York, 1968

The Good News: You're Not Crazy

1. Lamott, Anne. *Why I Make Sam Go To Church*. Traveling Mercies. Anchor Books (A Division of Random House), New York, 1999.
2. Tagore, Rabindranath. *Song 37*. Gitanjali A Collection of Indian Songs. MacMillan Publishing Co, Inc., New York, 1971.
3. Dillard, Annie. Teaching a Stone to Talk, Revised edition. Harper Perennial, New York, 1988.

Images For Our Lives

1. Meland, Bernard E. Fallible Forms and Symbols. Fortress Press, Philadelphia, 1976.
2. Scholefield, Harry. *Psychoanalysis and the Parish Ministry: Some Reflections on Unconscious Motivation in Preaching and Present Trends in Pastoral Counseling*. Berry Street Lecture, 1962.
3. Whitehead, Alfred North. Science and the Modern World (1925). Free Press (Simon & Schuster), 1997.
4. Franklin, R.W. The Poems of Emily Dickinson. Belknop Press of Harvard University Press, Cambridge, Massachusetts, 1999.
5. Booth, Philip. *First Lesson*. Letter from a Distant Land: Poems by Philip Booth. The Viking Press, 1957.
6. Langer, Suzanne. Philosophy in a New Key. Harvard University Press, Cambridge, 1963.
7. Sexton, Anne. *The Rowing Endeth*. The Awful Rowing Toward God. Houghton Mifflin Company, Boston, 1975.

8. Bandler, Richard and John Grinder. The Structure of Magic: Language and Therapy. Science & Behavior Books, Palo Alto, 1975.
9. Whitman, Walt. *Song of the Open Road* (Stanza 3). Leaves of Grass. Modern Library, New York.

Keep Your Lamps Trimmed And Burning

1. Gendler, J. Ruth. *Joy*. The Book of Qualities. Turquoise Mountain Publications, Berkeley, California, 1984.

You Do Not Have To Be Good

1. Oliver, Mary. *Wild Geese*. Dreamwork. The Atlantic Monthly Press, New York, 1985.
2. Barks, Coleman. The Essential Rumi. Harper Collins, San Francisco, 1995.

Spiritual, But Not Religious

1. Nouwen, Henri J.M. With Open Hands. Ave Maria Press, Notre Dame, Indiana, 2006.
2. Tirabassi, Maren. *The Living Pulpit (a* quarterly periodical, available through The Living Pulpit, Inc. 5000 Independence Avenue, Riverdale, New York).
3. Progoff, Ira. At a Journal Workshop. Dialogue House Library, New York, 1975.
4. Scholefield, Harry. A Walk on the Beach: Collected Sermons. First Unitarian Church of San Francisco, CA., 1999.

More than Enough

1. Mitchell, Stephen. A Book of Psalms. Harper Collins, New York, 1993 (p.52).
2. Cummings, E.E. *If touched*. Complete Poems, Revised edition. Liveright Publishing Corporation, New York, 1994.

What If You Knew Then, What You Know Now?

1. *Kunitz, Stanley. The Layers*. The Collected Poems. W.W. Norton & Company, New York, 2000.

America's Real Religion

1. Davies, A.Powell. America's Real Religion. Beacon Press, Boston, 1965.
2. Boston Globe, Friday, September 27, 1957, SectionD, p. 2. (Davies obituary)

3. Op Cit.
4. Ibid.

Marriage and Moral Values

1. Seaburg, Carl, editor. Great Occasions. Beacon Press, Boston, 1968.

It's Christmas Because it's Dark

1. Gilbert, Richard. *Practicing the Scales of Rejoicing.* Celebrating Christmas: An Anthology. Unitarian Universalist Ministers Association, 1983.
2. Auden, W.H. For the Time Being: A Christmas Oratio. Faber and Faber, New York, 1945.

It's About the Theology

1. Edgell, David P. *The Free Mind.* William Ellery Channing: Apostle of the Free Mind. Beacon Press, Boston, 1955.
2. Milford, Humphrey, editor. Poems of Emerson. Oxford University Press, London, 1914 (p.96).

Work It Out

1. Quindlen, Anna. *On Being a Mom.* Living Out Loud. Ballentine Books, New York, 2004.

Forgiveness

1. Remen, Rachel Naomi. My Grandfather's Blessings. Berkley Publishing Group, New York, 2000.
2. Kurtz, Ernest and Katherine Ketcham. The Spirituality of Imperfection. Bantam Books, New York, 1992.

Author's Note: Unless otherwise indicated, Bible passages are from The New Oxford Annotated Bible, Revised Standard Version. Herbert G. May and Bruce M. Metzger, New York, Oxford University Press, 1977.